Tell Your
Catholic
Friend

LEONARDO
DE CHIRICO

Tell Your Catholic Friend

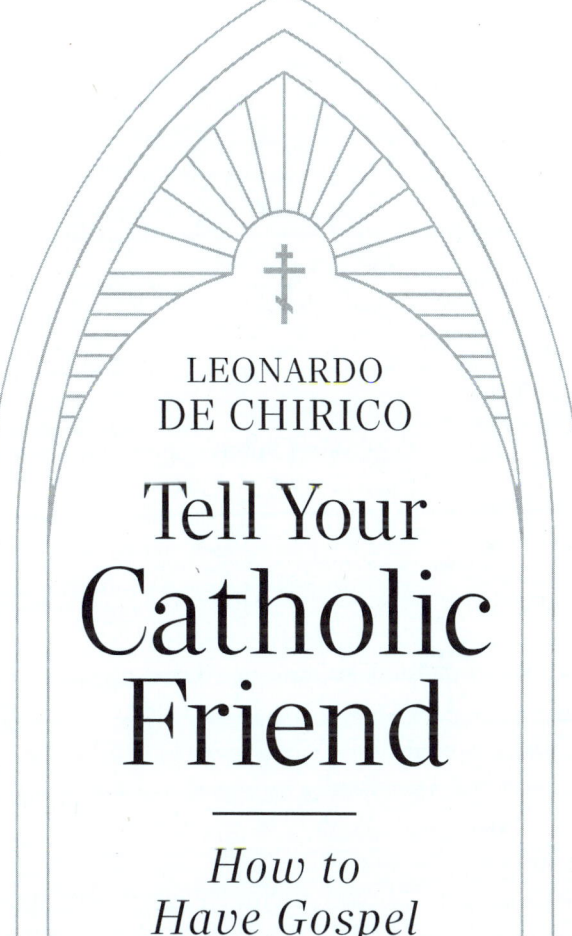

How to Have Gospel Conversations with Love

B&H PUBLISHING
BRENTWOOD, TENNESSEE

Copyright © 2025 by Leonardo De Chirico
All rights reserved.
Printed in the United States of America

979-8-3845-1608-8

Published by B&H Publishing Group
Brentwood, Tennessee

Dewey Decimal Classification: 282
Subject Heading: CATHOLICS / CHRISTIANITY

All Scripture is taken from the Christian Standard Bible. Copyright © 2017 by Holman Bible Publishers. Used by permission. Christian Standard Bible®, and CSB® are federally registered trademarks of Holman Bible Publishers, all rights reserved.

Cover design by Micah Kandros Design. Cover images by Vector Tradition, Richard Laschon, YummyBuum/Shutterstock. Author photo by Linda Acunto.

1 2 3 4 5 6 • 28 27 26 25

Dedication

I wish to dedicate this book to Paul and Gertrud Stilli. They are the Swiss missionary couple (serving with Operation Mobilization) whose story will briefly be told in chapter 2. In the late sixties they knocked on the door of my family apartment in Mantova, northern Italy, asking my father and mother two simple questions that God used to change their lives and, consequently, my life. (I was only a little child then.) They brought the gospel into our home, even though their mastery of the language was limited. They told their new Catholic friends the good news of Jesus. Their example of missionary zeal amid human vulnerability is what God used to impact my life. With this book, I want to encourage all believers to do what they did then: tell your Catholic friend!

Acknowledgments

I want to express my gratitude to the colleagues and friends of the editorial team of Loci Communes (www.loci-communes.it), a web magazine promoting evangelical culture in Italy since 2021. Sharing with our Italian Catholic friends insights and stories inspired by the gospel is also what lies at the heart of this book.

Contents

Introduction 1

Chapter 1: Roman Catholicism and the World
Your Friends Live In 9
    Three Reasons Why Roman Catholicism
        Is Far from the Gospel 10
    A Brief Definition of Roman Catholicism 13

Chapter 2: Being Born Again Is What Matters 33
    Who Is a Christian? 35
    The Cruciality of Conversion 45
    Thresholds of Christianity 49
    Old Issues, Yet Ever Relevant Ones 55

Chapter 3: Attitudes, Quadrants, and
Tips to Share the Gospel 63
    Finding the Right Attitude 65
    Using Keller's Atonement Grammars 68
    Applying Strange's Magnetic Points 72
    Four Tips to Share the Gospel 77

Chapter 4: FAQs as We Witness 87
   Should We Pray with Catholics? 87
   Can We Cooperate with the Roman
      Catholic Church? 91
   How Do We Debate with Catholics?. 95
   What about Our Similarities and Differences? . . . 100

Appendix 1: Christ Alone: A Sermon for All, Especially
Our Catholic Friends. 109

Appendix 2: Helpful Resources 117

Notes 119

Introduction

Let me introduce some of my friends.[1] Giulio is a high school teacher, much appreciated by students and colleagues for his academic expertise and sharp thinking. Every Sunday he goes to Mass and, if asked, would candidly identify himself as a Catholic. He is politically active as a left-wing campaigner, very supportive of every battle that has to do with "rights" (e.g., LGBTQ+ community, migrants). He was intrigued by Pope Benedict XVI's intellectual acumen but did not like his conservative stance on nonnegotiable values. During the week he attends a yoga class, and, in his apartment, he lights candles bought from the local new age shop to prevent evil spirits from entering. Occasionally, he participates in lessons led by a Catholic monk to improve his transcendental meditation.

Maria Pia is an aged, sweet, and generous lady. She is involved in the local Catholic parish on a weekly basis. Among the neighbors she is known as a religious and devout person. In her home she has pictures of the saints and of Our Lady (i.e., Madonna) to whom she prays regularly. Recently my wife had a sore throat, and when she shared her trouble with her, Maria Pia took from her kitchen cupboard a little bottle of olive oil that had been blessed in a shrine dedicated to St. Blaise, the patron saint of throats. She insisted that my wife dip her finger in it and massage her throat to be healed. In Maria's world, when she feels a need for something, it is to the saints and Mary that she turns for help. She says this is what her mother taught her, and this is what the church encourages her to keep doing.

Giacomo is a medical doctor who volunteers for a Catholic charity that helps the poor and destitute. He goes to Mass every day, often taking people with him, knowing that in the Eucharist they will really "encounter" Christ. He admires Pope Francis and his call to be an outward-looking church engaged in mission. He carries a copy of the New Testament in his bag, and his day is punctuated by prayers to Our Lady. When thinking about religions in general, Giacomo is open-minded. He believes that all people, especially the poor, are in one way or another recipients of divine grace, whether they profess Jesus Christ as their Savior and Lord or not, whether they receive the sacraments or not, regardless of their religion. He thinks we are "all brothers."

What do these friends have in common? Apart from being my friends in Rome, they are all Roman Catholics. All are baptized in the Roman Church, all partake of its sacraments, all feel a sense of belonging to it that is very much intertwined with their identity. Yes, they perform their religious life in different ways. When observed in their daily life, they believe different things and express what is most important to them in multiple forms. Yet to the question: "What's your religion?" they would all reply without hesitancy: "Roman Catholicism." They are different, yet they carry a shared identity. With different levels of intensity and integrity, Roman Catholicism marks their deep sense of who they are. With them I am in ongoing gospel conversations, trying to share the good news of Jesus Christ to them. This task is not easy but is worth pursuing.

I am sure my experience is not unique. We all know people who profess to be Roman Catholics. They may be friends, colleagues, family members, or neighbors. They may be practicing or nominal. They may be disconnected from their church or serious about their loyalty to it. They may be interested in starting a "spiritual" conversation or indifferent toward religious things. They may be progressive or conservative. They may be consistent with what they profess to believe or have their own "fruit salad" type of belief system where elements of Roman Catholicism are combined with Eastern religions or secular practices. This is to say that Roman Catholics can be very different people. How can we communicate the gospel to them?

I have been a pastor in Rome for fifteen years. Before coming to Rome, I have always ministered in a majority Catholic context in Italy, being engaged in church life, evangelism, discipleship, and training. In my more academic work, Roman Catholicism has been the topic I have studied much and written on. Interacting with Catholic friends, neighbors, books, and culture (i.e., theology and practice) has been the privilege and the challenge of my entire life.

In the city where the Holy See has its center and where the heart of the Roman Catholic Church lies, gospel ministry is as hard as elsewhere, with its unique features. Historically speaking, Rome was shaped by the Counter-Reformation—i.e., the opposition to the Protestant Reformation. The gospel that the city has been exposed to is a blurred and confused gospel. The personal reading of the Bible was forbidden, the control of the church on society was obsessive, the way people lived out their faith was and still is full of unbiblical elements. On top of this, the modern wave of secularism has added another layer of skepticism, thus making the resistance even greater.

Rome is even more unique because here the Catholic Church is also a political state (the Vatican), thus mixing religion and power. Rome looks like the city of Ephesus described in Acts 19, where the temple and business were intertwined in a shrewd alliance. Church buildings, church arts, church institutions, and schools are everywhere. Yet biblical Christianity is obscured. The standard Catholicism in Rome is deeply characterized by Marian and other devotions more than anything else. Roman Catholicism here is so culturally embedded (e.g., family ties, nationality) that it becomes undistinguishable from deeply felt personal and social identities. The cultural climate is skeptical, and so opportunities exist to introduce the gospel based on the virtuous circle of the proclamation of the gospel, personal witness, and church life. The latter is key to this goal because it joins believing and belonging, proclamation and service, the personal and the communal, creative contextualization and obedience to the Word of God. Along the way, I think I learned a few lessons on how to do it, although I am still learning.

This is why I wrote this book: to help people like you who are already involved in evangelism to Catholics or wish to be involved but don't know how to do it or where to start. This book will help you in your attempt to witness to your Catholic friends. It won't provide all the answers, but

INTRODUCTION

hopefully it will be a helpful tool to wrestle with the joys and challenges of being ambassadors of Christ to those Catholics who live around you.

How is the book going to be a resource? Hopefully in a fourfold way, as this summary of the chapters indicates.

First, it will sketch out a historical, theological, and spiritual map of Roman Catholicism: what it is, where it came from, and how it differs from biblical Christianity. If we encounter people who identify as Roman Catholics, it is important to have a bird's-eye view of the millennia-old and yet contemporary reality of Roman Catholicism: its institutional outlook, doctrinal framework, sacramental system, devotional practices, and global diffusion. Not all Roman Catholics have the same grasp of their own religious world, but all of them partake in it in some sense. To be able to present the gospel to them, we must at least be aware of what makes Roman Catholicism what it is. Moreover, the complexity of the various strands and regional faces of Roman Catholicism can easily lead to a partial and selected appreciation of what is at stake from a gospel viewpoint. Chapter 1 will provide a brief definition of Roman Catholicism and will also explain why, biblically speaking, it is not yet another Christian denomination but rather a deviation from biblical Christianity.

Second, the book will address the challenge we face in presenting the same biblical gospel to different types of Catholics. When we interact with our Catholic friends, we are talking with people who, while broadly comfortable to be identified with Roman Catholicism, embody that association in multiple ways. There is no single way of experiencing and manifesting the Roman Catholic faith. Each story is different because each person is unique. Despite this reality, one should not lose sight of the fact that, biblically speaking, we are ultimately either in Christ or outside of Christ. Either we are born again or not. It is important to be aware of different types of Catholics and to adapt our witness accordingly, yet we have the same gospel to share to people who are spiritually lost. People will not be saved because they are traditional, folk, charismatic, or secular Catholics, but by being born again by faith alone in Christ alone. This is what really matters.

Third, further zooming in, our journey will continue by exploring helpful attitudes and frameworks that can facilitate gospel conversations with our Catholic friends. Tim Keller's "expiation grammars" will be referred to as gospel narratives that can be useful connectors to people as we share the gospel. Then Dan Strange's "magnetic points" will also be briefly presented to test their suitability for our evangelistic efforts to Catholics. Gathering wisdom from these insights, I will suggest four tips to communicate the gospel that are sensitive to different contexts and individuals. They blend evangelical convictions and best practices that come out of my almost three-decades-long study of Roman Catholicism and my own experience in gospel witness to Catholics.

Finally, the last chapter will wrap up different threads in the book by asking (and possibly responding to) frequently asked questions that emerge in our relationship with Catholic friends. Can we pray together with them? Is it advisable to join arms in common action and evangelism? What happens if I am called to give a gospel talk to a majority Catholic

INTRODUCTION

audience? What questions do Catholic friends frequently ask in responding to the gospel, and what are the questions believers ask in witnessing to their Catholic neighbors? What tools can help in our conversations with Catholics?

Chapter 1

Roman Catholicism and the World Your Friends Live In

If we want to tell our Catholic friends the good news of Jesus, it is important that we have a sense of what Roman Catholicism looks like. Is it possible to define Roman Catholicism? Is it possible to capture the heart of the Roman Catholic worldview in a short description? Obviously "Roman Catholicism" is an extremely rich and complex universe. The risk of oversimplification, if not caricaturizing, is always a trap to be avoided.

Roman Catholicism's hundreds of years yet ongoing history makes it difficult to grasp its impressive historical trajectory. Its doctrinal outlook is the result of multiple stratifications and defies simplistic readings. Just a quick glance at the 1992 *Catechism of the Catholic Church* exposes a multifaceted and nuanced system of beliefs and practices that form its spiritual worldview. Its devotions reach into all spheres of life, shaping the entire human journey from birth to death. Its global reality embraces a huge variety of peoples and traditions, thus making it a true "catholic," universal body. At the same time, though, the "Roman" element is organically linked to it, tying the whole system to a very specific religious and political structure. Well-established ecclesiastical institutions are interwoven with dynamic movements. The Roman Catholic system is neither static nor monolithic but instead exists in an ongoing process of development, expanding without grounding itself ultimately in the teaching of Scripture. This is the world that our Catholic friends live in.

Three Reasons Why Roman Catholicism Is Far from the Gospel

The Presidential Address at the Evangelical Theological Society is a helpful barometer to measure where the wind blows in North American evangelical theology. In 2021, President Al Mohler dedicated his address at the 73rd annual convention in Fort Worth, Texas, to temptations confronting contemporary evangelical theology.[1] In Mohler's view, present-day evangelical theology faces four temptations: Fundamentalism, Atheism, Roman Catholicism, and Liberalism. These words are not to be taken lightly. The trajectory of evangelical theology has not always been peaceful; what is crucial is to understand the main dangers surrounding it.

Most interesting for this book is Mohler's inclusion of Roman Catholicism as one of the main temptations facing evangelical Christians. For centuries, Roman Catholicism was considered the theological antagonist of evangelical Christianity par excellence. In recent decades, however, this perception has gradually diminished, and the lines have become blurred. Today many evangelicals hold a very sentimental perception of Roman Catholicism. Some mistake it for one of the many Christian denominations, perhaps a little stranger than others; others, frightened by the increasing challenges of secularization, see Rome as a bulwark for defending Christian values; still others, perhaps seeking legitimacy at the ecumenical and interreligious table, overlook theological differences to highlight what appears to unite all.

The fact that Mohler says Roman Catholicism is a temptation and, therefore, a danger to beware of is a sign of spiritual vigilance. It indicates that even in the USA—where the confused, at best, initiative "Evangelicals and Catholics Together" has been underway since 1994[2] and where the differences between Catholics and evangelicals are increasingly seen as a question of nuance rather than substance—it is still possible to find evangelical voices calling for theological discernment.

The following are some of Mohler's statements regarding Roman Catholicism:

1. "To be evangelical is to understand that one of the questions we'll always have to answer is why we're not Catholic."

Mohler rightly argues that being evangelicals means *not* being Roman Catholics. The two identities are mutually exclusive. Either we are one or the other. Evangelical and Catholic theologies and practices arise from different basic convictions about God, the Bible, sin, salvation, the Christian life, etc. While using the same words, we refer to distant, sometimes opposite meanings. In recent years, on the

Catholic side, some have wanted to argue that it is possible to be "evangelical Catholics,"³ combining the two identities and making them compatible. Mohler says no. Either we are one or the other, and if we are one, we cannot be the other. The evangelical temptation is to adapt evangelical identity, but the result is denying it.

2. "I believe to go to Rome is to abandon the gospel of the Lord Jesus Christ. I believe it is to join a false church based on false and idolatrous presuppositions."

Roman Catholicism is not one of the many possible church options for a born-again believer in Jesus Christ who wants to grow and remain faithful to the Word of God. On the contrary, to follow Roman Catholicism is to go against the gospel in some sense. Rome's system is theologically flawed, and its church is spiritually misleading. These are strong words by Mohler, in contrast to the "ecumenically correct" language so common today. Yet, they are true words that must be said and repeated to avoid the temptation to go astray and lead others astray too.

3. "To be an evangelical is to recognize that we don't have a backstop. We have no alternative. We're left with the Bible alone and the Bible in its entirety as the Word of God."

For some evangelicals, the authority structure of Rome is a temptation in which they can find refuge. In a world where traditional institutions are shaking (e.g., family, nations, religions) and in which everything is in constant disruption, knowing that there is a magisterium, a pope, and a stable center can become very attractive. The evangelical faith, Mohler says, while part of the history of the faithful church and while cultivating a sense of belonging to the global church, is ultimately submitted to Scripture alone. An unwavering trust in the God of the Word and, therefore, in the Word of God is constitutive for the evangelical faith. Rome is no replacement for a lack of confidence in the Word of God and should not be a replacement for those whose faith is grounded in Christ alone based on Scripture alone.

A Brief Definition of Roman Catholicism

What can we say about Roman Catholicism as a whole? In recent decades, important heavyweights in Roman Catholic theology have helpfully contributed to the task of identifying the core of Roman Catholicism: think of Karl Adam (*The Spirit of Catholicism*, 1924),[4] Romano Guardini (*Vom Wesen katholischer Weltanschauung*, 1924),[5] Henri de Lubac (*Catholicism*, 1938),[6] Hans Urs von Balthasar (*In the Fullness of Faith: On the Centrality of the Distinctively Catholic*, 1975),[7] Walter Kasper (*The Catholic Church*, 2012),[8] just to name a few. The quest to single out the gist of Roman Catholicism is deeply felt within Roman Catholicism itself.

The best minds of contemporary Roman Catholicism have tried to analyze what is essential to Roman Catholicism. What can evangelical theology say about it? Can we participate in the discussion about the nature of Roman Catholicism from an outsider's perspective? In times marked by ecumenical correctness, can we say something that dares to be biblically critical?

Gospel conversations with Catholic friends are best served by transparency and honesty. It is more respectful to speak the truth in love than to hide it behind a screen of niceness that fails to address decisive issues, even if they are painful to discuss. With great approximation and a certain amount of courage given the complexity of the task, I suggest a provisional definition. Here it is:

Roman Catholicism is . . .

a deviation from biblical Christianity

consolidated over the centuries,

reflected in its Roman imperial institution,

based on an anthropologically optimistic theology and an abnormal ecclesiology

defined by its sacramental system,

animated by the (universal) Catholic project of absorbing the whole world,

resulting in a confused and distorted religion.

In suggesting this definition, we are addressing Roman Catholicism as a system from an evangelical viewpoint. We are not dealing with Roman Catholic people (more on this in the final section of the chapter), nor are we dealing with specific doctrines and practices.[9] Each line of the definition can be briefly explained.

A Deviation from Biblical Christianity

This definition contradicts a well-established narrative in the self-understanding of Roman Catholicism; namely, that Roman Catholicism is, due to the mechanism of apostolic succession, the legitimate and orthodox embodiment of apostolic Christianity. Others are schismatics (Eastern Orthodox) or heretics (Protestants), who broke the unbroken line of Roman Catholicism and strayed from its trunk. As was argued by the Protestant Reformers of the sixteenth century, this reading must be reversed. Roman Catholicism is not biblical Christianity in its original and apostolic form, but a departure from it. Its sacramental, hierarchical, and devotional developments were consolidated in its dogmatic structure, which took leave of the gospel. Roman Catholicism turns out to be a deviation hardened into an unbiblical dogmatic system (Marian dogmas, papal infallibility), intertwined with a political state (the Vatican), with which the church must not be confused. Roman Catholicism's public vision is more like the aspiration of an empire than the mission of the church of Jesus Christ.

In his *Treatise on the True Church and the Necessity of Living in It*, published in Geneva in 1573, the Italian Reformer Peter Martyr Vermigli (1499–1562) defended exactly this point: "we [the Protestants] did not leave the church, but rather went to the Church."[10] The Protestant Reformation was necessary to return to the gospel that the Roman system had corrupted. Biblical Christianity, never dormant in history despite the presence of multiple corruptions, experienced a new flourishing during the Reformation and subsequent Evangelical Awakenings.

As a deviation from biblical Christianity, Roman Catholicism is not even a legitimate denomination. Given that its dogmatic system (blurred at crucial points), its institutional structure (with a political entity at its core), and its devotional practices (many borrowed from paganism) have departed from the truth of the biblical gospel, the Roman Catholic Church cannot be considered one denomination among others. While evangelical Christianity has biblical standards by which it accepts Reformed, Baptist, Methodist, Lutheran, and independent congregations, among others, the Church of Rome belongs to another category. No denomination has a religious head and political leader; no denomination has irreformable dogmas with little if no biblical evidence; no denomination has an imperial structure like Rome. Therefore, Roman Catholicism is not one denomination among others.

Roman Catholicism relies on a mechanism of institutional succession that has guaranteed monarchical continuity from one pope to another through a well-refined system, but in its lack of adherence to the gospel of Jesus Christ and fidelity to the Word of God, it has embraced deviations that have become a self-referential system.

Consolidated over the Centuries

In addition to being a deviation from biblical Christianity, Roman Catholicism has consolidated over the centuries. There is no date of birth for Roman Catholicism, a precise moment to coincide with its beginning. Rather, there have been historical phases and transitions that have had a particular impact on its development.

The "Constantinian shift" of the fourth century was one of these key moments. In that century, Emperor Constantine granted religious freedom to Christians with the Edict of Milan (AD 313). However, he also gave financial and social benefits to the church to the point that she lost her independence and became integrated into the imperial system. The "Constantinian shift" culminated with the promulgation of Christianity as the religion of the Roman Empire by Theodosius I (AD 380). Christianity became part of what it meant to be a Roman citizen, and non-Christians were persecuted. The church gradually took on a Roman institutional form, increasing the power claims of the center over the peripheries. It was Roman bishops like Damasus I and Siricius who assumed for themselves the role of popes, which resembled that of an ecclesiastical emperor. Instead of being godly church leaders, pastors came to be associated with political stakeholders. After this crucial era, the imperial cloths taken on by the Roman Church have never been abandoned. On the contrary, they have been legitimized by an ecclesiology that has considered them part of the God-given nature of the church. The departure from the biblical form of the church—made up of converts to Jesus Christ, practicing the priesthood of all believers, in networks of churches connected but not within a hierarchical structure—was gradual, progressive and, tragically, irreversible for Roman Catholicism. Starting from the claims of authority by Damasus I and Siricius, Rome went on to claim for itself the "two swords" of government (spiritual and political) by

Boniface VIII (1230–1303). It took centuries to arrive at the dogma of papal infallibility of 1870, whereby the Pope was elevated to an infallible teacher when he would speak *ex cathedra* (literally, "from the chair," i.e., exercising his magisterial office). From the early developments after the "Constantinian shift" to the present-day outlook, the structure of the Roman Church has become imperial.

Another defining moment in Roman Catholic history was the development and reception of the title for Mary as "mother of God" (*theotokos*). The pronouncement in Ephesus (AD 431) that gave rise to an explosion of Mariology was twice elevated to the rank of dogma: in 1854, with the dogma of the immaculate conception of Mary, and in 1950, with the dogma of the bodily assumption of Mary. From a title intended to support the full divinity of Jesus Christ, Roman Catholicism has made Mariology an unbiblical pillar of dogmatic and devotional practice. This Mariology has repercussions on the Catholic doctrines of Christ, the Spirit, and the church; in short, it cascades over the whole of Catholic faith. This unorthodoxy has made Roman Catholicism porous to the absorption of pagan elements.

A third crucial moment was the Council of Trent (1545–63), when the Church of Rome officially rejected the message of the Protestant Reformation, anathematizing the call to return to the biblical gospel of salvation by faith alone in Christ alone based on the teaching of Scripture alone. "Tridentine" Catholicism, meaning the Roman Catholicism relaunched at Trent, has thickened the Roman departure from biblical Christianity, making it tougher and more unwilling to listen to the appeals of the Reformation—indeed consolidating its non-biblical commitments in every area of Christian theology, from the doctrine of salvation to that of the church, from Christology to spirituality.

Finally, the long parable of digressions cannot omit the last mile in the history of Roman Catholicism, the era following the Second Vatican Council (1962–65). Without denying anything of its past, the Roman Church has updated and further developed its doctrine and practice in a dialogical, absorbing, encompassing, but not purifying way. All the Roman structure of the past has been reaffirmed by juxtaposing it with a "Catholic" profile: soft, ecumenical, open to absorbing everything and everyone. To many, the changes introduced by Vatican II seemed like a real turning point; in reality, it was just a further stage in the self-centering of a system that does not want to reform itself according to the Word of God, but to relaunch itself in a new historical phase without losing any of its unbiblical tenets.

Reflected in Its Roman, Imperial Institution

The Roman Catholic Church presents itself as a hierarchical, top-down institution, divided between a restricted class of clerics and a large mass of laypeople. The sacrament of order is reserved for the former, alongside teaching and governing authority, while the latter are relegated to a sacramentally marginal role as executors. This division between a large base of laypeople and a small circle of clerics is against the biblical nature of the church, which is a body formed of various members all under one head, which is Christ, and at His service. The same hierarchical structure is found within the class of clerics, divided between parish priests, bishops, archbishops, and popes all in a hierarchical line. This imprint on the ecclesial institution is not biblical, but imperial. It reflects Roman imperial culture and its concept of the exercise of power, which have decisively forged the structure of the Church of Rome.

The papacy is the institution that best reflects imperial origin.[11] Even the most generous readings of Peter's role in the early church as described in the New Testament cannot justify the emergence of the papacy as the apical office of the church. Instead, the papacy resembles the office of the emperor, transposed to a religious institution. Many papal titles are ecclesiastical translations of imperial titles. Think, for example, of "Successor of the Prince of the Apostles (i.e., Peter)," "Supreme Pontiff of the Universal Church," "Primate of Italy," and "Sovereign of the Vatican City State." They are imperial titles. They are political roles. In the language used and in the culture they underlie, these titles are indebted to the politics of the Roman Empire, not to the exercise of responsibility in the church according to the gospel. Where does the Bible speak of a human head of the church who is "prince," "pontiff," "primate," even "sovereign" of a state? It is clear that we are in the presence of a transposition of titles that are alien to the church of Jesus Christ because they derive from the political ideology of a human empire.

Think of how the recent *Catechism of the Catholic Church* (1992) defines and describes the role of the Roman Pope. In paragraph 882 it says that "the Roman Pontiff, by reason of his office as Vicar of Christ and as Pastor of the entire church, has full, supreme and universal power over the whole church, a power which he can always exercise unhindered."[12] Full, supreme, and universal power—this is an imperial power not defined by Scripture, which, on the contrary, limits all powers inside and outside the church. See paragraph 937, where we read: "The Pope enjoys, by divine institution, supreme, full, immediate, and universal power in the care of souls."[13] Power is still talked about and defined in imperial terms, except to attribute it to the divine will!

The papacy is the child of an imperial conception, at the top of which is the emperor (pope) surrounded by a senate of aristocrats (cardinals and bishops) who govern free men (priests) and a mass of slaves (laymen). Roman Catholicism assumed the imperial structure and reproduced it in its own self-understanding and internal organization. The tragedy is that it also clothed this imperial structure with a divine *imprimatur* as if it descended directly from God's will, making it unchangeable. Any attempt to biblically justify the imperial structure of the church is an afterthought, trying, in vain, to see Roman Catholicism as the organic development of the New Testament church. Instead, the Church of Rome is the daughter of the Roman Empire. When the empire fell, from its ashes emerged the ecclesiastical structure that has perpetrated its ideology for centuries, up to the present day.

Based on an Anthropologically Optimistic Theology and an Abnormal Ecclesiology

At the foundation of Roman Catholic theology lie an anthropologically optimistic theology and an abnormal ecclesiology, the two main axes of the whole Roman Catholic theological system.

The first axis concerns the relationship between nature and grace or, as Gregg Allison usefully called it in his book *Roman Catholic Theology and Practice: An Evangelical Assessment*, the "nature-grace interdependence."[14] Roman Catholicism recognizes God's creation (nature) and has a sense of God's grace. Nature exists, just as divine grace exists in relation to it. What is lacking in this scheme is a biblical, and therefore realistic, understanding of sin. In a biblical worldview, the first act of creation is followed by the second act, the breaking of the covenant between God and humanity caused by sin. This second act has devastating and cascading effects on all of life. Roman Catholicism, though it maintains a doctrine of sin, does not have a biblically radical one. While it considers sin a serious illness, it does not consider it spiritual death. For Roman Catholicism, nature, before and after sin, is always *capax dei* (i.e., capable of God), intrinsically and constitutively open to the grace of God.

For this reason, Roman Catholicism is pervaded by an attitude that is confident in the capacity of nature to objectify grace (the bread that becomes Christ's body, the wine that becomes Christ's blood, the water of baptism, and the oil of anointing that convey grace), in a person's ability to cooperate and contribute to salvation with his or her own works, in the capacity of other religions to be ways to God, in the capacity of the conscience to be the point of reference for truth, and in the capacity of the Pope to speak infallibly when he does so *ex cathedra*. In theological terms, according to this view, grace intervenes to elevate nature to its supernatural end, presupposing its untainted capacity to be elevated. Even if weakened by sin, nature maintains its ability to interface with grace because grace is indelibly inscribed in nature. Roman Catholicism does not distinguish between common grace, with which God protects the world from sin, and special grace, with which God saves the world. Therefore, Roman Catholicism is pervaded by an optimism that whatever is natural can be graced.

The second axis of Roman Catholic theology deals with the relationship between Christ and the church. In Allison's terms, it is the "Christ-church interconnection." Roman Catholicism teaches that after the ascension of the risen Jesus Christ to the right hand of the Father, there is a sense in which Christ is really present in His "mystical body," the church, which is inseparably connected to the hierarchical and papal institution of the Roman Church. For Roman Catholicism, the incarnation of Christ did not end with the ascension but is continued in the sacramental, institutional, and teaching life of the church. The Roman Church exercises the royal, priestly, and prophetic offices of Christ in a real sense: through the priests who act *in persona Christi*, the church governs the world, dispenses grace, and teaches the truth.

The prerogatives of Christ are thus transposed to the church: the power of the church is universal, the sacraments of the church transmit grace *ex opere operato*, by reason of them being enacted, and the magisterium of the church is always true. The biblical distinction between the head of the body, Christ, and the members of His body, the church, is confused by the Roman Catholic category of *totus Christus*, the total Christ which includes both. The consequences of this confusion pollute how the church conceives itself and how it operates. The mystical-sacramental-institutional-papal church is conceived in an inflated, abnormal way.

Roman Catholicism functions within these two axes: the underlying optimism, based on an interdependence between nature and grace, and the leading role of the Roman ecclesiastical institution, based on the interconnection between Christ and the church.

Defined by Its Sacramental System

The sacramental system is the true operational infrastructure of Roman Catholicism. Sacramentality refers to the idea of mediation: since nature is intrinsically capable of being elevated by grace, grace is not received immediately or externally, but always through a vehicle. Divine grace is communicated to nature through sacraments. From the Roman Catholic sacramental point of view, the grace of baptism is imparted with water, the grace of extreme unction with oil, the grace of order with the imposition of hands, and the grace of the Eucharist with consecrated bread and wine. Grace cannot be received by faith alone but always through a natural element imparted by the church, which acts in the name of Christ and transforms it from a merely natural element to the "real presence" of divine grace.

Therefore, two elements are necessary for a Roman Catholic sacrament: a physical element and the agency of the church, which is believed to have the task of transfiguring matter and imparting grace. The interdependence between nature and grace means that grace comes into nature and through nature; the interconnection between Christ and the church means that the Church of Rome dispenses it in the name of Christ Himself. Since it is Christ who works through the sacraments of the church, they have an effect *ex opere operato*, by the very fact of being imparted, making the recipient's trust in Christ and repentance from sin secondary.

The Council of Trent (1545–63) designed the sacramental layout of the Church of Rome, from baptism to extreme unction, in response to the Protestant Reformation, which had emphasized that the work of Christ is received by faith alone through the work of the Holy Spirit. The layout is made up of seven sacraments—baptism, confirmation, confession, Eucharist, order, marriage, extreme unction—that accompany human life from birth to death. The Roman Church dispenses God's grace in every stage of life. Some sacraments are administrations of grace received once and for all, such as baptism, confirmation, order, marriage, and extreme unction, while others are received cyclically and repeatedly, such as confession and the Eucharist. In this way, God's grace becomes real and pervasive through the action of the church. For the Council of Trent, being excluded from the sacraments by excommunication, schism, or belonging to other religions was equivalent to being excluded from grace.

While not denying the Tridentine system, the Second Vatican Council (1962–65) added an important emphasis. The last Council shifted attention from the sacramental acts of the Catholic Church to the sacramental essence of the church. In the famous conciliar definition, "the church is in Christ like a sacrament or as a sign and instrument both of a very closely knit union with God and of the unity of the whole human race" (*Lumen Gentium* 1). Thus, the church itself is a sacrament, that is, the "real presence" of Christ. The church expresses unity with God and accomplishes the unity of the whole human race. For this reason, Rome can speak of everyone as brothers and sisters. Those that Trent considered excluded from grace, because they were excluded from the sacraments, the Church of Rome now considers as brothers and sisters already impacted by grace, albeit in a mysterious way, and already in some way ordained to the Catholic Church. From the sacraments as specific acts to the sacramentality of the church as a whole, this is where the Roman Catholic Church stands today.

The gospel recognizes the goodness of creation but also the radical nature of sin. The natural man does not receive the things of the Spirit if they are not revealed to him (1 Cor. 2:12–15). The flesh or sinful nature does not receive grace; it is the Spirit who gives life (John 6:63). Jesus instituted the ordinances of baptism and the Lord's Supper as "visible words," according to the beautiful expression of the Italian Reformer Peter Martyr Vermigli,[15] that testify to the grace received by faith, not as objects through which grace is made present by a church that believes itself to be the extension of the incarnation of Jesus Christ.

Animated by the (Universal) Catholic Project of Absorbing the Whole World

The Apostles' Creed describes the church as "catholic" in the sense of universality, extending throughout the world, but the meaning given to catholicity by the Church of Rome goes beyond the universality of the church.

Following the conclusion of Vatican II, the Italian Protestant theologian Vittorio Subilia published a book in which Vatican II's approved documents were examined and in which an overall interpretation of the Roman Catholicism that emerged from the Council was provided.[16] The Roman Catholicism of Vatican II has given up theocratic claims inherited from the long centuries of its history and, instead, invested heavily in increasing its catholicity. It can no longer think of dominating the world in an absolutist way, so it seeks to permeate the world and modify it from the inside. It no longer hurls anathemas against modernity but strives to penetrate and elevate it. It no longer imposes its power coercively but tries to exercise it gracefully. The Church of Rome lacks a strong popular following when it speaks of doctrine and morals, so it tries to maintain its ability to influence, condition, and direct society indirectly. It can no longer afford a wall-to-wall contest with the world; in order not to be relegated to a nook, it accepts modern society in order to permeate it from within.

In a military metaphor, it can be said that the tactics of Roman Catholicism are no longer those of a head-on collision but of the wrapping of the wings. The goal isn't annihilation but incorporation. The aim isn't conquest but absorption through the expansion of the boundaries of catholicity. Everything falls within the jurisdiction of Roman Catholicity.

This new catholicity lies in the ability to incorporate divergent ideas, different values, and heterogeneous movements, integrating them within the Roman system. If the evangelical faith chooses Scripture alone, Christ alone, and faith alone, Roman Catholicism doesn't argue against them but adds to them—Scripture and tradition, Christ and the church, grace and sacraments, faith and works. In fact, Roman Catholicism has such a broad framework that it can accommodate everything, a thesis and its antithesis, one instance and another, one element and another.

In the Roman Catholic worldview, nature is conjugated to grace, Scripture to tradition, Christ to the church, grace to the sacraments, faith to works, Christian life to popular religion, evangelical piety to pagan folklore, speculative philosophy to superstitious beliefs, ecclesiastical centralism to Catholic universalism. The biblical gospel is not its parameter; therefore, Roman Catholicism is always open to new integrations in its progressive expansion.

The basic criterion of Roman Catholicism is not evangelical purity nor Christian authenticity, but the integration of any particular into a universal horizon at the service of a Roman institution that holds the reins.

Resulting in a Confused and Distorted Religion

Now that we have examined the various elements of my definition of Roman Catholicism, it is time to close the circle by reaching a provisional conclusion. So what can be said about the doctrinal outlook, the devotional patterns, and the institutional structure of Roman Catholicism as a whole? Roman Catholicism can be said to be a confused and distorted religion.

Its "formal principle," or source of authority, is not Scripture alone but the Word of God alongside the church's tradition, which ends up falling under the teaching office of the Roman Church. Not having Scripture as the ultimate authority, Roman Catholicism can only be biblically confused, ambiguous, and, ultimately, erroneous. Each of its main uses of Scripture, however linguistically adherent to the Bible, is crossed by a principle contrary to the Word of God.

Its "material principle," or primary teaching, is not the grace of God received by faith alone which saves the sinner, but a sophisticated system that merges divine grace with the performance of a person through the reception of the sacraments of the church. Roman Catholicism speaks of sin, grace, salvation, and faith. Yet it employs these words not according to their biblical meaning but by bending them according to its own sacramental system. The words are the same but, not being defined by Scripture, their meaning is fraught with internal divergence. They are phonetically equal but theologically different from the Christian faith.

Some distortions of Roman Catholicism are obvious, such as Marian dogmas without biblical support, acts of devotion drawn from pagan practices, and the institution of the papacy, which is the child of the Roman Empire. Others are subtler and more sophisticated, including doctrinal developments that have accrued over the centuries and Roman Catholic ecclesiology and teaching on salvation.

In light of these pervasive distortions, even what appears to be held in common with biblical Christians must be carefully questioned. As the document "An Evangelical Approach Towards Understanding Roman Catholicism" of the Italian Evangelical Alliance says:

> The doctrinal agreement between Catholics and Evangelicals, which is expressed in a common adherence to the Creeds and

Councils of the first five centuries, is not an adequate basis on which to say that there is an agreement concerning the essentials of the Gospel. Moreover, developments within the Catholic Church during the following centuries give rise to the suspicion that this adherence may be more formal than substantial. This type of observation might also be true of the agreements between Evangelicals and Catholics when it comes to ethical and social issues. There is a similarity of perspective which has its roots in Common Grace and the influence which Christianity has generally exercised in the course of history. Since theology and ethics cannot be separated, however, it is not possible to say that there is a common ethical understanding—the underlying theologies are essentially different. As there is no basic agreement concerning the foundations of the Gospel, even when it comes to ethical questions where there may be similarities, these affinities are more formal than substantial (n. 9).[17]

How are we to relate to Roman Catholics as individuals and groups? Again, the same document helpfully argues:

> What is true of the Catholic Church as a doctrinal and institutional reality is not necessarily true of individual Catholics.

> God's grace is at work in men and women who, although they may consider themselves Catholics, trust in God alone, and seek to develop a personal relationship with him, read the Scriptures and lead a Christian life. These people, however, must be encouraged to think through the issue of whether their faith is compatible with membership of the Catholic Church. They must be helped to examine critically residual Catholic elements in their thinking in the light of God's Word (n. 12).[18]

Our Catholic friends will be on different sides of the Roman Catholic spectrum. Some will be more consistent with the *Catechism of the Catholic Church*, others less so. Some will be closer to the gospel than others. Yet all women and men are called to return to God the Father, who manifested Himself in the person and work of Jesus Christ through the power of the Holy Spirit, to be saved and to relearn how to live under the authority of the Bible for the glory of God alone.

This is what we want to tell our Catholic friends!

Chapter 2

Being Born Again Is What Matters

My father was a devout Roman Catholic. While he didn't regularly attend Mass, he seriously engaged in Catholic practices. He was a fan of Saint Antony, a Portuguese medieval saint. He had a picture of the saint in his wallet. He kissed it before going to bed. He made pilgrimages to the tomb of the saint in Padua every year. He felt part of the Roman Catholic Church. He accepted that the church was there to deal with his religious life, so he could carry on with living, only making sure to receive the sacraments occasionally and to pray to the patron saint. God was too remote for him, too distant, too otherworldly to be known and approached. The church was, therefore, the mediating agency he could rely upon. Saint Antony was the saint he felt near to. My father's life was religiously respectful but spiritually empty, full of devotion yet void of the gospel. This is what Roman Catholicism had taught him. His heart was restless, and God was far away.

One day our family was visited by a missionary couple from Switzerland. They could hardly speak Italian, yet they were courageous enough to engage in a gospel conversation with Italians. At the doorstep, they had enough confidence to ask two simple and searching questions: "Are you Christians?" The answer was simple. "Yes, of course; we are Italians!" my parents replied with a hint of surprise. Being Italian was the same as being Christian. The second question was: "Have you ever read the Bible?" Turning to my mother in puzzlement, my father replied, "Dear, do we have a Bible at home?" "No, dear," she said. This was a mark of traditional Roman Catholicism, especially before Vatican II—a lack of biblical literacy and a life filled with traditions and practices often contrary to plain and simple biblical teaching. Reading the Bible was the beginning of a journey that led both my dad and mom to become born-again Christians. Soon after, my older brother and I followed.

My story is one of personal and family reformation according to the gospel. This has been the story of millions of former Roman Catholics around the world who were raised in a religious tradition with little or no exposure to the Bible and with inaccurate ideas about the gospel. They thought they were Christian because they had been baptized, but they were not born again. They were rescued by discovering the message of the Bible and the good news of salvation in Christ alone received by faith alone. This was the medicine for the salvation of my family. This is why we must tell our Catholic friends about Jesus.

Who Is a Christian?

The word *Christian* can mean different things to different people and can be used in different contexts.[1] When approached by the missionary couple, my father was asked the question and his answer was: "Yes, of course; I am Italian!" For him, being a Christian equaled being Italian and vice versa. In his answer, a whole theology of Christian identity was implied. Being a Christian was associated with national identity rather than biblical markers. Spirituality and citizenship were blurred to the point of overlapping. While reading Scripture and being exposed to the gospel, my father came to terms with the unsatisfactory nature of his answer. Was his Christian identity defined by him belonging to a culture and nation historically and culturally shaped by a form of Christianity or was there something radically different to grapple with?

My father's answer is indicative of the mindset of many of our Catholic friends. Not all of them will link Catholicism to their national and cultural identity, but all of them will think that they are Christians because they were baptized in the Catholic church. At best, they are nominal Christians. How do we try to help them realize that, biblically speaking, being a Christian means being born again? Let's have a look at what the Bible says about what it means to be a Christian.

The Perimeter of the Name

"The disciples were first called Christians at Antioch" (Acts 11:26). Followers of Christ had been around for some time before the Antioch episode is mentioned, as Antioch is not the first Christian church in the book of Acts. Before Antioch there was Jerusalem, Samaria, Damascus, Lydda, and Caesarea. In the geographic development of the church, the city of Antioch was reached in the context of a progressive dissemination of the gospel. Antioch, however, has a particularity among ancient Christian churches. It is a church that functioned as a link between the initial expansive phase of the early church, marked by daring and unexpected movements, and the more intentional path of ongoing church growth. Antioch stood between a somewhat forced mission and a more deliberate mission.

Chapter 11 tells how the gospel arrived in Antioch. For the first time, the disciples were called Christians. Other names in the religious vocabulary were still useful but no longer fully adequate.[2] The church was, for example, composed of Jews and non-Jews, and the Jewishness of the group was no longer sufficient to describe it fully. Since many of these disciples were not Jews, nor did they belong to another single group, ethnic markers were insufficient to describe them. The name "Christian" denoted not so much an individual identity, but the social reality of a new community marked by a common faith in a common Lord.

The text also tells us that meetings in Antioch were held regularly for a whole year, which communicates continuity and stability in the community's life. The Christians are described as having a spiritual and communal identity marker for a prolonged length of time. It is after the observation that this community is relatively stable and taking residence in the city that their religious profile begins to take shape. With such identifiable and clear contours, it required lexical creativity to single them out. A new word was born: the disciples were therefore called "Christians." This word described a phenomenon that could no longer be described with previously existing words. It could not be described in opposition to something else but needed a new name to be properly identified on its own terms. The word *Christian* was not applied an artificial way. It arose from the evidence of a now-public identity. "These people are Christians!"

A couple observations about the name. First, a Christian is associated with being a disciple. *Disciple* is the standard New Testament word indicating someone who follows the teaching and example of a master. The disciple is not only one who is cognitively on the same page with the teacher, but one whose life is also spiritually and existentially identified with the master. Any sense of detached or superficial Christianity is therefore excluded. In calling people to become disciples of Jesus Christ, Christianity is a totalizing religion, a call to embrace the path of the Master to the point of identifying oneself with the death and resurrection of the Lord Jesus (Rom. 6:4). The word used in Acts 11:26 is plural, "disciples." One is not a disciple on her own. Disciples are called to be a community of followers. Christianity is an all-embracing life program that one needs to pursue personally and in fellowship with other like-minded, fellow disciples. Christianity is, therefore, a radical faith in terms of its demands and expectations, and it is a social faith at its very heart.

Second, the name "Christian" bears a pervasive reference to Christ. It is a lexical construction (*Christianoi*) based on the name of Christ. His name is stretched to the point of becoming a descriptor of His disciples. So deep is the identification between Christ and Christians that His followers who bear His name are people who can affirm together with the apostle Paul: "For me, to live is Christ" (Phil. 1:21). Christ defines their identity so pervasively that His name is the one they bear.

On the whole, then, the naming of these disciples of Christ did not follow a cheap, shallow, or superficial definition of the phenomenon. It was rather the contrary. The name reflected that Christianity involved the whole of life: a belief system associated with the message of Christ, ethical behavior that stemmed from the example of Christ, and belonging in the community of the followers of Christ. Belief, behavior, and belonging: in its programmatic meaning, these three dimensions mark the content of the name "Christian." In J. I. Packer's lucid summary, "being a Christian is a blend of doctrine, experience and practice. Head, heart and legs are all involved. Doctrine and experience without practice would turn me into a knowledgeable spiritual paralytic; experience and practice without doctrine would leave me a restless spiritual sleepwalker."[3]

Going back to the origins of the name, the word *Christian* is not an empty box that can be arbitrarily filled according to various spiritual inclinations and preferred options. Though it is open to personal, ecclesial, and cultural embodiments, it retains a fundamental core that needs to be accepted as a given, shaped how the Bible intends. This givenness of the name forms the nonnegotiable, biblically defined DNA of what it means to be a Christian.

Interweaving different biblical threads about the identity of a Christian, "The Lausanne Covenant" (par. 4) puts its range in pentagon figure. The name "Christian" fills a space whose contours are:

1. Commitment to the historical, biblical Christ as Savior and Lord.
2. Repentance and reconciliation to God.
3. Acceptance of the cost of discipleship in following Christ, denying self, and taking up the cross.
4. Incorporation into Christ's community, the local church.
5. Engaging in responsible service in the world for Christ.[4]

In other words, to be a Christian is to be committed to the historical Jesus Christ (faith as *notitia*) as one's own personal Savior and Lord (faith as *assensus*) in repentance and faith (faith as *fiducia*). The name "Christian" also has an inherent connection to discipleship and a cruciform, Christlike life. Christianity is quintessentially lived out within the church and in the world in service and mission. The markers of Christian identity may vary in intensity and in their overall balance. Christians may have different levels of awareness of their identity or different degrees of understanding of what it means to be a Christian.

There is no hint of sacramental language, though. Baptism cannot define what a Christian is. Contrary to Roman Catholic and ecumenical views, whereby baptism *causes* repentance and faith, the Bible acknowledges the importance of baptism in the context of a personal response to the gospel.

Approximations and Boundaries around the Name

The name "Christian" did not originate in a vacuum and was not left as an empty space for people to fill in arbitrarily. It emerged as a descriptor of a specific spiritual, personal, and communal reality, marked by the identification of the followers of Jesus Christ with the Master. In the New Testament, the name "Christian" is never considered an over-spiritualized ideal, nor an abstract concept. While it has a stable perimeter and a Christlike shape, it is always connected with real people in the real world struggling to walk through the ups and downs of their Christian life.

The Bible acknowledges that Christians live different approximations of the identity carried in their name. Christians may be weak (Rom. 14:1) or strong (Rom. 15:1), thus indicating various degrees of spiritual strength and depth in living out the Christian life. Christians can live in different stages and phases; they can be spiritual children doing childish things and then become adults (1 Cor. 13:11) with more mature postures in their understanding of the faith. A childish Christian still depends on milk, elementary teaching of the Word of God, whereas a mature one can be fed by solid food (Heb. 5:12–13) in order to better discern good and evil. Spiritual childhood can also lead to worldly, contentious, and immature performances of the Christian life as opposed to spiritual maturity which displays the mind of Christ (1 Cor. 3:1–3). Christians are urged to warn the idle, encourage the timid, and help the weak (1 Thess. 5:14), because these conditions are real and well represented in the church. People carrying the name "Christian" find themselves at different stages of maturity in their spiritual journey. This is the reason why each apostolic letter is replete with exhortations, admonitions, and encouragements addressed to believers to move forward in the Christian life and away from dangerous pitfalls or regressive trends. While all Christians share the same positional status before God that allows them to be identified with Jesus Christ, Christians bear witness to and embody this identity in a variety of ways.

In his usually neat and profound language, John Stott provides a useful summary of how the biblical gospel gives rise to legal and positional dimensions received by the believer as a disciple of Christ, as well as originating a renewal process leading to transformation and maturity. The gospel of salvation

> denotes God's total plan for man, and it includes at least three phases. Phase one is our deliverance from the guilt and judgment of our sins, our free and full forgiveness, together with our reconciliation to God and our adoption as His children. Phase two is our progressive liberation from the down-drag of evil, beginning with our new birth into the family of God and continuing with our transformation by the Spirit of Christ into the image of Christ. Phase three is our final deliverance from the sin which lingers both in our fallen nature and in our social

environment, when on the last day we shall be invested with new and glorious bodies and transferred to a new heaven and a new earth in which righteousness dwells. Further, these three phases, or tenses, of salvation (past, present, and future) are associated in the New Testament with the three major events in the saving career of Jesus, His death, His resurrection and subsequent gift of the Spirit, and His return in power and glory. Paul calls them justification, sanctification, and glorification.[5]

From Stott's summary, the basis of Christianity appears to have a threefold significance: a legal dimension whereby the person is freed from the guilt of sin and justified by grace, a transformative dimension whereby the person experiences conversion into new life and becomes part of the people of God, and an eschatological dimension whereby the effects of sin will be eventually wiped out and the shalom of God will reign forever. As far as the first dimension is concerned, it is an either/or condition that is received by grace alone through faith alone. It is the ground of the Christian life, the entry point into God's kingdom, the threshold of salvation. As for sanctification, it is an ongoing process that leads to progressive approximations of Christian maturity. All Christians, already justified by faith alone, are called to walk through the journey of growth and service.

This is all to say that the name "Christian" should be associated with those who belong to Christ, having been justified and adopted by God. While justification marks the position, the status, and the standing of the Christian before God, sanctification points to the renewal and gradual, progressive process of transformation that takes place in the life of the Christian. The former is characterized by the *hapax* adverb (once and for all, definitive) as it is used to describe the finality of the work of Christ on the cross in Hebrews 9:28; the latter is by the *mallon* adverb (ever more, ongoingly) as it is used to indicate the progress in the Christian life in 1 Thessalonians 4:10.[6]

Simply put, Roman Catholic Christianity retains the name "Christian" but requires a reinterpretation of its meaning. The heart of what it means to be a Christian is blurred to the point of being altered. Some of our Catholic friends will tell us that Christianity is a matter of being born into a given family, belonging to a cultural or religious context, or having undergone a Christian initiation process that has little to no impact on one's daily life. For nominal Christians, being a Christian may only be a passing inference, superficial, remote, and peripheral. They are Christian by name but not in reality, practice, or belief. They feel they belong to something associated with Christianity with various degrees of proximity; what they actually believe and the way it is reflected in their lives is a much more complicated matter. In terms of the belief system, many of my Catholic friends have a kind of patchwork, selective theology based on a self-made version of the Christian faith that does not square with the biblical witness. The same eclecticism is true in their moral vision and practice, where secularization can be found in their private and public lives, all while retaining degrees of religious language or concern. More radically, these nominal Christians lack experiential engagement and spiritual participation in the biblical definition of what it means to be a Christian. They tend to lack any evidence of being disciples of Jesus according to the Antiochene blueprint.

As mentioned previously, my father considered himself a Christian because he belonged to a national and cultural community loosely associated with a form of Christianity inherited by tradition, not by being a disciple of Jesus Christ in the biblical sense. He felt as if he belonged to something without believing the gospel and striving to behave accordingly.

The definitions of nominal Christianity may vary considerably, and their complexity should be fully appreciated. Here is how the Lausanne Occasional Paper 10 defines a nominal Christian:

> A nominal Christian is a person who has not responded in repentance and faith to Jesus Christ as his personal Saviour and Lord. He is a Christian in name only. He may be very religious. He may be a practising or non-practising church member. He may give intellectual assent to basic Christian doctrines and claim to be a Christian. He may be faithful in attending liturgical rites and worship services, and be an active member involved in church affairs. But in spite of all this, he is still destined for eternal judgment (cf. Matt. 7:21–23, Jas. 2:19) because

he has not committed his life to Jesus Christ (Romans 10:9–10).[7]

This definition lays out some important points. A nominal Christian has not yet undergone personal conversion to Christ through repentance and faith. His allegiance to the name of Christ is still impersonal and remote. Christ may be an important figure but not the Lord and Savior of his life. She may express various degrees of religiosity, even practicing forms of Christian devotion and liturgical participation. Furthermore, he may even be active in a church body and contribute to its life. On their own, a generic religiosity, an apparent spirituality, formal membership in a church, even an evangelical church, and involvement in its activities are not signs that biblical Christianity is present. Signs of inherited cultural religiosity are not in themselves spiritual evidence of a regenerated life and, therefore, cannot be equated with Christianity according to the gospel.

The Cruciality of Conversion[8]

A biblical understanding of the name "Christian" is characterized by insistence on the personal need for salvation and the personal responsibility to respond to God's grace in repentance and faith. The gospel is both an announcement of God's intervention to save and a summons to respond in faith. Using David Bebbington's terms, *conversionism*, together with *Biblicism*, *crucicentrism*, and *activism*, captures the heart of evangelical Christianity, because it recognizes the centrality of a personal encounter with Jesus Christ that results in forgiveness of sin and a changed life.⁹ The Reformation doctrine of salvation based on *solus Christus*, meaning "in Christ alone," is matched by the revivalist emphasis on the necessity of personal conversion. Against the view that evangelicalism and its gospel-centrality is only a child of modernity, Stott argued that evangelicalism is not "a new-fangled 'ism', a modern brand of Christianity, but an ancient form, indeed the original one."[10]

Jesus's injunction to Nicodemus, "You must be born again" (John 3:7), becomes paramount for all people. Regeneration through conversion is the necessary threshold both for salvation and to be recognized as a Christian, and it is achieved by the Holy Spirit through the preaching and witness of the gospel to which people respond in repentance and faith.[11] Salvation does not come by simply being born into a Christian family, nor from being part of a Christian environment. Not even being a formal member of a Christian church nor having received a sacrament of Christian initiation can earn salvation. It is not by merit, it is not by works, it is not by tradition, it is not by sacraments; it is by grace alone through conversion to Jesus Christ. This is what our Catholic friends need to hear!

Reflecting on the centrality of conversion in an evangelical account of initiation into the Christian faith, Stephen Holmes writes: "Evangelicals are those who preach the same gospel of punctiliar conversion and immediate assurance available through faith alone."[12] This is not to suggest that there is a single pattern or timing of conversion. In this respect, Klaas Runia correctly says, "When it comes to the 'form' of conversion, there are some differences of opinion among evangelicals (is conversion instantaneous, so that one can mention time and place, or is it more in the nature of a process?), but generally evangelicals do not prescribe a particular method or a particular manifestation. The emphasis is on the fact of conversion, not on its particular form."[13]

The fact of personal conversion is what really makes the difference in answering the question: Who is a Christian, and who is not? Most converted Christians can identify with the words of John Newton (1725–1807), who in his world-famous hymn "Amazing Grace" could write:

> I once was lost, but now am found,
> Was blind but now I see.[14]

Personal stories may vary considerably, but they are all characterized by personal conversion. Biblical Christianity according to the Antiochene blueprint is a conversionist religion, and every Christian should to be ready to share her personal "testimony," the account of her or his conversion and personal walk with the Lord.

The objective message of the cross is the legacy of the *sola* principles of the Reformation. This together with the personal experience of salvation, forms the foundation of much evangelical preaching of the gospel, especially of those sermons that came out of the various revivals of post-Reformation history. J. I. Packer and Thomas Oden are helpful here when they write: "Evangelicalism characteristically emphasizes the penal-substitutionary view of the cross and the radical reality of the Bible-taught, Spirit-wrought inward change, relational and directional, that makes a person a Christian (new birth, regeneration, conversion, faith, repentance, forgiveness, new creation, all in and through Jesus Christ)."[15] John 3:16 is the single Bible verse where the gospel of God's salvation and man's responsibility to believe are masterfully condensed. Christians champion, memorize, and extensively use John 3:16 in their spiritual pilgrimage and personal evangelism because it combines the love of God manifested in Christ with the response to it shown in personal faith.

Stemming from the Antiochene blueprint of Christianity, modern revivals reflect the long trajectory of church history by placing an emphasis on personal conversion as the necessary step toward salvation. This stress on conversion has strongly influenced evangelical preaching of the gospel that invites people to repent from sin, believe in Jesus as personal Savior and Lord, and be saved, urging people to respond and to walk through a conversion experience. The "sinner's prayer" captures important features of the contemporary evangelical account of conversion and the expectation of transformation it will produce.

> Lord Jesus, I need You. Thank You for dying on the cross for my sins. I open the door of my life and receive You as my Savior and Lord. Thank You for forgiving my sins and giving me eternal life. Take control of the throne of my life. Make me the kind of person You want me to be.[16]

The vocabulary of conversion is by no means exclusive to the evangelical tradition. It belongs to the shared language of all branches of Christianity, because it is a biblical word. However, evangelicals tend to understand conversion as a *hapax*, the Greek adverb meaning a once-and-for-all turning to God in repentance and faith, attaching to it a salvific dimension and assurance of salvation, while other traditions, including Roman Catholicism, tend to understand conversion as part of an ongoing religious journey and a call for daily renewal. An unconverted Christian may be an oxymoron, but one needs to be clear about what conversion to Jesus Christ means and how it affects one's life.

Thresholds of Christianity

Reflection on conversion needs to be taken a step further. Evangelicals tend to view conversion in relational categories, whereby God saves lost sinners in reconciling them to Himself by the work of Christ alone. The whole theological vocabulary of salvation is relational in focus and intent: regeneration (life language), justification (juridical language), adoption (familial language), and conversion (change language). These are all pictures that depict the reenacted relationship between God and man in different ways. Contrary to Catholics, evangelicals find it difficult to conceive of salvation in sacramental terms. In the evangelical understanding and experience of salvation, the sacraments are important but not prominent. They are in the background, of course, as part of the God-given and Scripture-attested life of the church, but they are not essential to salvation or to defining who is a Christian and who is not.[17] The sacramental dimension of Christianity is "second without being secondary."[18]

To put it simply: no born-again Christian would say that she is a Christian primarily because she has been baptized or because she is a regular participant at Communion services. The historic view of Christianity is that salvation is God's free gift, in spite of us, through the work of Jesus on the cross and His resurrection, appropriated by faith. John Stott is again helpful here:

> If there is no saving merit either in our good works or in our faith, there is no saving merit in the mere reception of the sacraments either. . . . It is not by the mere outward administration of water in baptism that we are cleansed and receive the Spirit, nor by the mere gift of bread and wine in Communion that we feed on Christ crucified, but by faith in the promises of God thus visibly expressed, a faith which is itself meant to be illustrated in our humble, believing acceptance of these signs. But we must not confuse the signs with the promises which they signify. It is possible to receive the sign without receiving the promise, and also to receive the promise apart from receiving the sign.[19]

The cross, not baptism or the Eucharist, takes center stage in conversion.[20] The *hapax* (once-and-for-all) significance of the cross is emphasized much more than the *hapax* of baptism or the *mallon* (more and more) aspects of the Eucharist.[21] Each church tradition has its own view of the sacraments, but they should not lie at the center of their faith, nor does sacramental language define the grammar and vocabulary of the biblical understanding of what constitutes the core of being a Christian.

Linked to evangelical uneasiness toward sacramental language is the place of the church in defining biblical Christianity. Being a Christian means having responded in repentance and faith to the gospel through the unique mediation of Christ; the church is a creature of this event. The emphasis should be placed on the direct relationship between a person saved and Christ, rather than on the church as a corporate agent that administers grace.

Stemming from the once-and-for-all work of Christ and the firm promises of the gospel, Christians can experience a high degree of assurance of salvation. Salvation is certain because of the juridical significance of justification and the eschatological trustworthiness of God's covenant promises. "If I die today, I will go to heaven" is standard evangelical language. Sometimes this attitude is perceived as arrogant and misplaced by our Catholic friends, yet it reflects the "grace alone," "faith alone," and "Christ alone"—Reformation emphases of what it means to be a Christian. Indeed, salvation belongs to the Lord, and those who receive it can be assured of it, despite their failures. Non-evangelical Christians often find it difficult to appropriate this assurance, and their reluctance derives from a different way of understanding the nature of Christianity and who is a Christian.

Yet another critical side of this issue deserves attention. In present-day Roman Catholic Christianity, heavily influenced by interfaith dialogue and universalist trends of thought,[22] the discussion about nominal Christianity has taken a new trajectory.

The Roman Catholic Church used to be committed to a strict and traditional interpretation of the dictum *"extra ecclesiam nulla salus,"* meaning that outside of the church there is no salvation. Those who did not sacramentally and juridically belong to the Roman Church, both non-Catholic Christians and non-Christians following other religions, were not considered to be Christians in the proper sense. The Second Vatican Council (1962–65) significantly changed the Catholic understanding of the meaning of this dictum, giving rise to a "gradualist" view of Christianity.

Vatican II documents explain the change in status of non-Catholic believers, just as non-Christian religions are also seen in a new light. People who follow other religions, even if far away from Christianity, are no longer considered away from Christ. They are, instead, in some measure related to Christ (*Lumen Gentium*, n. 16), whether they wish it or not, whether they know it or not. If we take into account the fact that, according to the council, Catholics enjoy a privileged relationship with Christ, being incorporated with Him (*Lumen Gentium*, nn. 11, 14, 31), Roman Catholicism is seen as a completion, the achievement of aspirations that are already existing in non-Christian religions. The grace of God is already present in other religions, and the church, because of its special prerogatives, is the place where they can be exalted to their accomplishment. In this post–Vatican II view, every man and woman is mysteriously associated with the "Paschal mystery" (*Gaudium et Spes*, n. 22). Clearly, the catholicity of present-day Roman Catholicism, which has much in common with an ecumenical theology of religions, transcends the narrow boundaries of Christianity as defined by an explicit faith in Jesus Christ and a distinct journey of Christian discipleship.

Roman Catholic theologian Karl Rahner's "anonymous Christianity" is an example of this position:

> Therefore no matter what a man states in his conceptual, theoretical, and religious reflection, anyone who does not say in his heart, "there is no God" (like the "fool" in the psalm) but testifies to him by the radical acceptance of his being, is a believer. . . . And anyone who has let himself be taken hold of by this grace can be called with every right an "anonymous Christian."[23]

Anonymous Christianity means that a person lives in the grace of God and, therefore, is a Christian whether or not he is aware of it; he attains salvation "outside of explicitly constituted Christianity."[24]

Christianity is today perceived in many Roman Catholic circles in a gradualist view, giving rise to different shades of what it means to be a Christian. All people are included in one way or another in the circles of Christianity. This development may be trendy and politically correct, but it is fundamentally wrong. The gradualist interpretation of Christianity blurs the covenantal nature of the Christian faith and transforms it into a universalist religion that has little to do with the Antiochene blueprint. In today's world, dialogue between Christian traditions must be a means of elucidating these differences with biblical clarity and frankness.[25]

To wrap up, "The Lausanne Covenant" is again worth quoting to bring this section to a close.

> To proclaim Jesus as "the Saviour of the world" is not to affirm that all people are either automatically or ultimately saved, still less to affirm that all religions offer salvation in Christ. Rather it is to proclaim God's love for a world of sinners and to invite everyone to respond to him as Saviour and Lord in the wholehearted personal commitment of repentance and faith (n. 3).[26]

And again:

> The goal should be, by all available means and at the earliest possible time, that every person will have the opportunity to hear, understand, and to receive the good news (n. 9).[27]

Hearing, understanding, and receiving the gospel: these are what define a Christian. A Roman Catholic Christian may have come close to hearing, understanding, and receiving the gospel. He may have received the sacraments, but he is not a Christian unless he is born again. In our gospel conversations with Catholics, our task is to facilitate under God and in all ways possible the proclamation and witness of the gospel to them.

Old Issues, Yet Ever Relevant Ones

I want to take you now to the city of Rome in 1511 to tell another story of personal conversion. A young German monk, Martin Luther, visited the eternal city that year. He came as a pilgrim to immerse himself in devotional practices in the hope of finding peace for his troubled soul. Apart from the corruption that he witnessed in the church there—undermining the credibility of the clergy and its teachings—Luther saw that the gospel that dominated Rome was encapsulated in the Holy Stairs next to the basilica of St. John the Lateran. There pilgrims would climb the stairs on their knees, praying Marian prayers, and after reaching the top, they would pay a certain amount of money to receive an indulgence.

An indulgence was and remains a remission of sin granted by the Catholic Church to the faithful one who performs a good work. In special years, called holy years or jubilee years, the Roman Church dispenses indulgences more lavishly. Luther came in one of those holy years. The basic concept of indulgences is that God is far removed from you. In order to reach Him you have to do a combination of good works, such as prayers, pilgrimages, and offerings, and then the church will dispense God's forgiveness on His behalf. You must climb the steps of heaven in order to fulfill the requirements of the church, which will then open for you the storage of divine grace. Luther was troubled when he saw this practice. Something was wrong about the whole thing. He would soon after discover that the entire system advocated by the Roman Church was ill-formed, confusing, and distorted.

It is not true that we must reach out to God with our works, ascending the ladder of heaven, trusting that the church will mediate God's forgiveness to us. The Bible clearly teaches that it is God who, in His Son Jesus, has come down to us to make atonement for our sins. The whole scheme was wrong and needed to be turned upside down. Therein lay the essence of the Reformation; after being exposed to the biblical gospel, the Reformers turned the trajectory of salvation right-side up. The Son descended to us in His incarnation. He died for our sins and rose from the dead for our salvation. We are called to believe in Him.

The problem with Roman Catholicism in the sixteenth century is still the problem with present-day Roman Catholicism. The same Holy Stairs that Luther saw are there, every day packed with people kneeling on their way up to look for God's forgiveness. It has been going on for centuries without any significant change and it's still going on today. Why?

The Bible Is Not the Ultimate Authority

The main problem with Roman Catholicism is that its doctrines and practices are not based on the Bible alone, but on the Bible and the traditions of the church. Both the Bible and the traditions are then interpreted by the teaching office of the church. The Bible is not the final authority. The church, who embodies tradition and interprets the Bible, is.

Roman Catholicism acknowledges Scripture to a certain extent, but it affirms its own traditions at the same time. The Bible is one of its authorities but not the only one, nor the highest. In Roman Catholic doctrine (see, for instance,

Vatican II: *Dei Verbum*), God's revelation comes to us in oral tradition that takes two forms: the written text of the Bible and the living voice of the official teaching of the Roman Catholic Church. According to this view, tradition is prior to the Bible, bigger than the Bible, and its present-day voice is not primarily the biblical text but the ongoing teaching of the church. The Bible cannot be the ultimate authority. Therefore, it cannot teach, reproof, correct, and train if it's not the final word. There is something bigger than it, and there is something more relevant than it, the tradition that the church gives voice to. According to Roman Catholicism, the Bible is important but inconclusive. It is one form of revelation but not the final one.

One example may suffice to illustrate how the Catholic system works. Take, for instance, the doctrine of Mary, or Mariology. The Bible gives us a sober account of the mother of Jesus. However, listen to how the Roman Catholic Church has developed it: "the Blessed Virgin is invoked by the church under the titles of Advocate, Auxiliatrix, Adjutrix, and Mediatrix" (Vatican II: *Lumen Gentium*, n. 62). These are all Christological titles that were passed onto Mary. What the Bible ascribes to Jesus alone, the Roman Church ascribes to Mary. Why? Because tradition takes precedence over the Bible and can, therefore, lead to these Mariological developments that detract attention from the Lord Jesus. It is no surprise that in many majority Catholic regions, the cult of Mary is more practiced than praying to Jesus. It is no surprise that the motto of Pope John Paul II was *totus tuus*, totally yours, with "yours" referring to Mary. It is no surprise that Pope Francis has a strong Mariological spirituality. Every day he prays the Marian rosary, and he speaks about her often. As already mentioned, having a final scriptural warrant is not the point for the Catholic faith. The Bible is not conclusive. Tradition is instead determinative and conclusive, and the church is considered the living voice of God's revelation.

Salvation Is Not by Faith Alone

In Roman Catholicism, since the Bible is not the ultimate authority, its genetic code is inherently disordered. The source of authority has been displaced from the written Word of God, so a second fundamental problem arises in Roman Catholic teaching and practice with respect to the problem of humanity and how one is reconciled to God. In other words, the issue of salvation is at stake.

The Roman Catholic Church rejected the biblical doctrine of salvation by faith alone at the Council of Trent (1545–63). Trent continued to use the word *justification* but filled it with a different meaning. For Trent, justification was a process rather than an act of God—a process initiated by the sacrament of baptism, where the righteousness of God was thought to be infused; a process nurtured by the religious works of the faithful and sustained by the sacramental system of the church; a process often requiring a time of purification in purgatory, before perhaps being enacted on judgment day. Rome reframed and reconstructed justification in terms of a combination of God's initiative and man's efforts, grace and works joined together, resulting in an ongoing journey of justification, ultimately dependent on the "clay and iron" of human works and ecclesiastical sacraments. Missing is the declarative, forensic act of justification, the exclusive grounding in divine grace, the full assurance of being justified because of what God the Father has declared, God the Son has achieved, and God the Spirit has worked out. Trent formalized a confused and confusing teaching on justification that has been misleading people ever since.

The gospel of Rome is, therefore, built on these blurred foundations: the Bible is not the final authority, and salvation is not by faith alone. This is the core of the theological disorder of the Catholic Church.

Why the Reformation Is Not Over

There are two biblical options for dealing with those who claim to be Christians, preach the gospel, and yet differ from us: Philippians 1:15–18 and Galatians 1:6–9. The first passage speaks of those who may have wrong motivations and evil attitudes ("envy" and "rivalry"), but the heart of the matter is that they proclaim Christ. For Paul, in spite of suffering from these bad behaviors, the fact that they preached Christ was ultimately a matter of rejoicing. Galatians 1 paints a radically different picture. The people who preached in this passage may be nice and charming, but they proclaim a different gospel that distorts the gospel of Christ. In both options what is really at stake is the truth of the gospel that is proclaimed. One can be harsh with other Christians, but if he or she preaches the gospel, it is a matter for rejoicing. Others may seem gentle and merciful, yet they preach a false gospel. The question we must ask of all who claim Christ and differ from us, including Roman Catholics, is which of these two passages best describes them.

The church will continue to be founded on the ultimate authority of Scripture and justification by faith alone. There is no other recipe available for a healthy gospel church. There is no other gospel than the biblically attested message of Jesus Christ that saves unworthy sinners like us on the basis of His once-and-for-all work on the cross. The Bible is crystal clear that we are either justified by God's grace or we fall in a kind of self-justification that is a tragic deception. Any accommodation to the idea that we are ultimately dependent on the authority of the church or capable of saving ourselves, any accommodation of the claim that salvation is not God's gift from beginning to end, is a slippery slope toward a false gospel.

As the 2016 statement "Is the Reformation Over?"—signed by dozens of evangelical theologians and leaders worldwide—argues:

> In all its varieties and at times conflicting tendencies, the Protestant Reformation was ultimately a call to (1) recover the authority of the Bible over the church and (2) appreciate afresh the fact that salvation comes to us through faith alone.[28]

These are the standing and unresolved disagreements between Roman Catholics and evangelical Protestants.

Present-day Roman Catholicism has tried to come to terms with the Reformation by expanding its synthesis, redefining terms, and becoming friendlier to those outside its walls, but not by changing its doctrinal core. The theological disorder of Rome remains, and this is why the Reformation is an ongoing task, as urgent today as it was five hundred years ago.

Because of the massive number of Roman Catholics around the world—around 1.3 billion people—there is a high probability we all have neighbors, friends, family members, and colleagues who are Catholic. Wherever you are in the world, Roman Catholics are likely to be your next-door neighbors. Many Catholics believe and behave like Western secular people do, without any sense of God being real and true in their lives. In other words, they are not born-again, regenerated Christians. Devout Catholics may be religious, yet they are entangled in traditions and practices that are far from the biblical faith. This presents us with wide-open evangelistic opportunities. The gospel can and must be taken to them too. We must try to enter the Roman Catholic mindset to gently challenge it with the gospel.

Chapter 3

Attitudes, Quadrants, and Tips to Share the Gospel

In his letter to the Colossians (4:3-4), the apostle Paul asked for prayer that God would open doors for him to be able to share the gospel and that he would be able to explain it clearly and appropriately, as he should. He desired discernment and wisdom so that he could communicate the gospel in a way that made sense to his hearers. We see this desire put into practice in Paul's interaction with the Athenians (Acts 17), when he contextualizes the gospel for his hearers. In his book *Center Church*, Timothy Keller defines contextualization as follows:

> Giving people the answers in the Bible, which they may not want to hear, to the questions about life that people in their particular time and place are asking, in a language and form they can understand, and through appeals and arguments with force they can feel, even if they reject them.[1]

Paul was not alone in contextualizing the good news of the kingdom of God. A quick reading of the Gospel according to Luke shows us that Jesus also spoke in ways that revealed an intimate knowledge of His context, using language and stories that made sense to His listeners. Preachers contextualize every Sunday when they use illustrations that help listeners to better understand what Scripture teaches us.

Contextualizing the gospel does not mean adapting the gospel to the culture, as if the message needs to be changed. Rather, it is about conveying the gospel message with an awareness of the context in which it is shared so that it can be understood. Contextualization leads to compromise when one tries to unite the gospel to the culture through syncretism. There is the danger of under-contextualizing, when we are so blinded by our own experiences that we always start from our cultural framework and do not modify it for our listeners. There is also the danger of over-contextualization, when we change the gospel message to fit today's cultural narratives and thus distort it, usually out of a desire to be appealing to the culture. We all need to be aware that we risk falling into one of these dangers. How can we avoid them? By an unwavering commitment to the gospel.

Paul wrote to the Corinthians saying:

> To the Jews I became like a Jew, to win Jews; to those under the law, like one under the law—though I myself am not under the law—to win those under the law. To those who are without the law, like one without the law—though I am not without God's

law but under the law of Christ—to win those without the law. To the weak I became weak, in order to win the weak. I have become all things to all people, so that I may by every possible means save some. Now I do all this because of the gospel, so that I may share in the blessings. (1 Cor. 9:20–23)

What we really want to do through contextualization is to show our Catholic friends that what they seek can only be found in Christ. As Keller says, "We show listeners that the plots of their lives can find a composition, a 'happy ending,' only in Jesus."[2] In an upcoming section we will look at an example of various "grammars" or "languages" of the atonement that can help to us share the gospel message to Catholics.

Finding the Right Attitude

In any attempts at sharing the gospel with Catholic friends, Chris Castaldo's *Talking with Catholics about the Gospel* is a poignant resource.[3] Castaldo helps us to come to terms with the different subcategories of Catholics that one may encounter. He explains that there are "traditional Catholics," "evangelical Catholics,"[4] and "cultural Catholics." Each category has its own way of living out their Roman Catholic identity, and each one brings with it specific challenges and opportunities in terms of gospel witness. This typology can be refined according to whichever context one finds oneself in. Ray Galea talks about a spectrum from "ultra-conservative and traditionalist" Catholics critical of Vatican II to mainstream Catholics who broadly follow Vatican II, liberation theology Catholics, generally left-wing political liberals, and folk Catholics, shaped by the particular subculture they were born into.[5] In my corner of the world in Rome, Italy, I find some traditional Catholics and many cultural Catholics, but I also meet with people whose Catholicism is largely characterized by folk-religion practices like devotions to the saints and the cult of the dead. I am unsure which category they fit best, perhaps Castaldo's "cultural Catholics" or Galea's folk Catholics. Whatever terminology you introduce, there will always be people who don't completely fit it.

What is even more interesting is Castaldo's focus on evangelical attitudes. His book provides a helpful taxonomy of evangelical approaches to Roman Catholics. They range from "actively anti-Catholic" to "passively anti-Catholic"; from "co-existent" to "positive identity"; from "symbiotic" to "ecumenical" to "internal renewal." Each approach is based on different evaluations of Roman Catholicism, based on a mix of knowledge and experience. As someone willing to reach out to his Catholic friends, the reader may find it a helpful exercise to place himself in one of these categories in order to be aware of his spiritual motifs, theological convictions, and personal experiences with Catholics.

Our attitudes should be marked by what the apostle Peter tells us to do when we give a "reason for the hope" that is in us: "do this with gentleness and reverence" (1 Pet. 3:15–16). Among other things, this means that we should not spend time unfairly attacking Catholic beliefs and practices or criticizing the Roman Church as the primary goal of our conversations. Evangelism always has an apologetic edge, but it should be done in kindness in such a way that your attitude and posture reflect the gentleness and respect that Peter is talking about.[6]

To cultivate the right posture marked by Christian love, Gregg Allison shares wise advice in his chapter titled "How Can I Talk with My Catholic Loved Ones about the Gospel?": "Concretely, we may express our love as prayer for them and on their behalf. What are their needs and burdens? Let's pray for them and for those matters."[7] Prayer should always be part of what we do as witnesses of the gospel.

Another significant chapter in Castaldo's book is devoted to clarifying the theological issues at stake by expounding "similarities and differences" between evangelicals and Catholics. There are multiple doctrinal divergences, but the ultimate point of difference, says Castaldo, lies in the contrasting view of the incarnation of Christ as it is related to the nature and mission of the church. Here he quotes Joseph Ratzinger, Pope emeritus Benedict XVI: "The notion of the body of Christ was developed in the Catholic Church to the effect that the church designated as 'Christ living on earth' came to mean that the church was described as the Incarnation of the Son continuing until the end of time."[8] Understood in this way, the church assumes the prerogatives of Christ in His roles as prophet, priest, and king. His prophetic role becomes the magisterial office of the church. His priestly role becomes the sacramental structure of the church. And His kingly role becomes the political authority of the church. From this fundamental difference, other divergences emerge in relation to authority, salvation, the perpetual sacrifice of the Mass, purgatory, indulgences, veneration of the Saints, penance, and the mediating role of Mary.

Behind history and doctrines, however, are real people with their stories and beliefs, and this is too often overlooked in evangelism. All true disciples of Jesus Christ must be actively involved in personal witness of the gospel and do it in ways that embody the good news. Any evangelistic effort toward Catholics should occur under the biblical rubric of "grace and truth." If personal evangelism is not done in grace and truth, it does not honor God or advance the cause of the gospel.

Using Keller's Atonement Grammars

As already seen, contextualization seeks to communicate the gospel by relating it to the deepest desires of our listeners and making an appeal for them to understand and respond. How can we appeal to people in our contexts when there are different influences on them, shaping how they think about the world and their values? We can use many of the themes that the Bible shares.

The Bible includes such diversity that its message can be related to any cultural narrative we may find in our friends. The Bible speaks of sin and salvation using the language of exile and return, the temple, God's presence and sacrifice, covenant and faithfulness, kingdom and victory. Keller provides a useful tool for our gospel appeals using the Bible's "grammars" or "languages" of the atonement, with the understanding that the atonement is the reconciliation between God and humanity accomplished through the work of Jesus Christ. These grammars can help us to share the gospel message in particular ways with particular people.

Here are the languages, or grammars, through which Christ's work of salvation on the cross can be presented:[9]

1. *The language of the battlefield.* Christ fought for us against the forces of sin and death. He defeated the forces of evil for us.
2. *The language of the slave market.* Christ paid the ransom price, bought us, paying our debt. He frees us from slavery.
3. *The language of exile.* Christ was exiled and cast out of the community so that we who deserve to be banished can be welcomed. He leads us back home.
4. *Temple language.* Christ is the sacrifice that purifies us and makes us fit to approach the holy God. He makes us pure and beautiful.
5. *The language of the court of justice.* Christ stands in the presence of the judge and takes upon Himself the punishment we deserve. He takes away our guilt and makes us righteous.

Thinking of our Catholic friends, which grammar is the most fitting in our gospel conversations? Temple language may be an obvious one. Catholics, especially practicing ones, are used to the sacraments of the Eucharist and reconciliation and to a sacramental understanding of their lives more generally that involves temple imagery. For them the church is the temple that administers God's grace to people. It is through the sacraments of the church that they can become holier. It is through the priest that their encounter with God is made sacramentally possible. Their life happens in a temple setting that is filled with saints, dead and alive, with whom they can talk. If this is their context, we can use temple language to present Jesus Christ Himself as the true temple (John 2:21) and the High Priest who has done all that was necessary for our salvation (Heb. 4:14–16). He is the only Mediator between God and humanity (1 Tim. 2:5) and the One who receives our prayers (John 14:14). Thus, temple grammar may resonate more than others with Catholics.

The language of the court of justice is less familiar to present-day Catholics, who are not used to framing their relationship with God in terms of justification by faith and the biblical language of imputation and reckoning. They may need explanation to grasp the gravity of sin and the forensic significance of Christ's sufficient work for sinners apart from human works (Rom. 3–5). The court language could be reframed away from a works-based understanding to a biblical, legal setting, whereby Christ's righteousness is extolled, and substitutionary atonement is magnified.

The language of exile takes a particular form in Catholic culture, especially if your friend has been immersed in an honor-shame culture. Especially among an older generation of Catholics, a sense of guilt can be strongly perceived, and it gives rise to fluctuating feelings of either being guilty for all the things they do wrong—therefore going to church to seek sacramental restoration—and disregarding the rules all together. The good news that Jesus took our shame by bearing our sins (Heb. 12:2) is truly liberating. Because of what He has done for us, we can be confident that our sins are forgiven (Rom. 8:33–37) and that our honor is restored.

As for the other grammars, they may apply depending on specific life circumstances. It is important to familiarize yourself with all of them in order to articulate the gospel in a relevant way, depending on the person you are talking with. Having said that, sometimes we think we can choose one grammar and ignore the others, but that is not the case. Each way of presenting the atonement reflects a part of Scripture and reveals a unique aspect of our salvation, but we can benefit by using more than one grammar. Furthermore, what do they have in common? They all share the central theme of substitution. Regardless of the grammar used, Jesus acts as our substitute. Jesus fights evil for us, pays the price for our salvation, and takes our punishment. Jesus is our substitute! Keller wrote that "the single theme that brings the greatest consolation and speaks to everyone's heart is substitution."[10]

Jesus's sacrificial work guarantees a happy ending! These grammars can be adapted to the challenges and desires of each person, and the different languages used will resonate with various people and cultures. For example, the language of the battlefield and the slave market appeals to those who fight oppression and desire freedom. The language of the temple and the court of justice addresses those who seek relief from guilt and shame. Think of all the people in our cities who are doing penance. The language of exile speaks to those who feel alienated and rejected. (Think of, perhaps, minorities and immigrants in our neighborhoods, among others.)

So I challenge you to learn these grammars. Consider which ones are most relevant in your context and how they can be used in your relationships and church life to proclaim the good news of Jesus, the perfect substitute!

Applying Strange's Magnetic Points

Besides applying Tim Keller's grammars, I have also found it useful when talking to Catholic friends to reference the five "magnetic points" expounded by British theologian Daniel Strange.[11] They are five fundamentals that all human beings are looking for and to which they are magnetically drawn. Because of their universal presence in people's lives, they can be seen in Catholics.

According to Strange, each religion responds in various ways to these five questions. Their responses are points of attraction for people to be drawn to them. The questions are:

1. The search for totality: a way to connect to reality?
2. The need for a norm: a way to live?
3. The yearning for deliverance: a way out of oppression?
4. The sense of destiny: a way to control?
5. The reality of a higher power: a way to measure up to the supernatural?

According to Strange, "these magnetic points act as a kind of 'religious anatomy' of fallen human beings."[12] Other religions suppress God's truth and seek to substitute it with an alternative account, resulting in a messy combination of beliefs and practices. According to Strange, every religious conversation touches on one or more magnetic points. It is up to us to succeed in conveying the message of the gospel by showing how the good news is the right answer for relating to the world, living according to God's will, being set free from sin, relying on divine benevolent providence, and living in the power of the Holy Spirit.

Every religion, Roman Catholicism included, provides improbable and insufficient answers to the magnetic points. The gospel subverts these answers and fulfills the magnetic points. In the darkness of human existence, only the proclamation of the gospel of Jesus Christ can bring light. Truth is found in Him. This is the complete and living power for people, the power long suppressed and rejected. Dan Strange comments: "The gospel of Jesus Christ does not bypass the magnetic points, but is the subversive fulfillment of the magnetic points."[13] The gospel does not replace the points but presents a Person, Jesus Christ, who fulfills them and grants them to those who believe; in fact, "our hope is not in a 'what' but in a 'who'."[14] Here is how He does it.

1. *Totality.* Jesus says, "I am the vine; you are the branches. The one who remains in me and I in him produces much fruit" (John 15:5). He connects us to Himself, freeing us from our isolation.

2. *Norm.* Jesus says, "Don't think that I came to abolish the Law or the Prophets. I did not come to abolish but to

fulfill" (Matt. 5:17). He provides a moral norm for life and death, based on His own character, without degrading into moralism.

3. *Deliverance.* Jesus says, "I am the way, the truth, and the life" (John 14:6). He alone brings a finished deliverance; we cannot perform it ourselves and are liberated from guilt and shame.

4. *Destiny.* Jesus says, "I am the good shepherd. The good shepherd lays down his life for the sheep" (John 10:11). For those who trust Him, their destination is not enslavement, but wholeness in resurrected bodies.

5. *Higher power.* Jesus says, "I am the light of the world. Anyone who follows me will never walk in the darkness but will have the light of life" (John 8:12). He is the Highest Power who became a human being we can know and love personally.

It is up to the church to be a magnetic people, living out the gospel in a way that testifies to God's authority, God's control, and God's presence in and over everything. In our conversations with friends, Strange suggests four moves to employ the magnetic points:

1. entering our neighbor's world
2. exploring his belief system
3. exposing its weaknesses and faults
4. evangelizing by presenting Jesus, always communicating the gospel "holistically and humanely"[15]

As already noticed with Keller's grammars, Strange's magnetic points also apply specifically to our gospel conversations with Catholic friends. A few examples can be briefly mentioned, especially as far as the points related to totality, norm, and higher power.

Totality

Roman Catholicism provides a sense of belonging to a bigger story and community. Catholics feel a part of something historical, global, cultural, and institutional. Unfortunately, the totality Roman Catholicism offers is not grounded in the biblical gospel and has multiple cracks in it. Often Catholics become disillusioned with the institution, develop skepticism, and look for totality either in family traditions that are embedded in religion or in secular options. Jesus Christ grants a far better and deeper identity. He gives us a place in His historical and global family. In biblical terms, we become a branch among many grafted into the vineyard (John 15:5), living stones within the spiritual house (1 Pet. 2:5), ears of wheat in God's field (1 Cor. 3:9), sheep within an innumerable flock (John 10:16), members never disconnected from the whole body (1 Cor. 12:27). Without neglecting the particular identity of each person, the biblical vision is strictly collective. In short, submitting to Jesus's leadership as our head involves becoming members of His body (1 Cor. 12:12). As a community of believers, the church, as imperfect as it is, is nonetheless our spiritual home where fellowship and support can be found.

Norm

Over the centuries, Rome has developed a detailed moral code for the faithful. There are norms for all aspects and moments of life, often presented in moralistic terms. To be a good Christian, you must perform these norms as your duty. In our contemporary world, many Catholics want to be disentangled from the moral framework of the church. They experience it as cumbersome if not oppressive, an imposed and impersonal code. The opportunity is there for us to present Christ as the One who fulfilled God's requirements and gives the good life we long for but cannot find apart from Him (John 10:10). Christ's truth liberates us and gives us the desire to follow Him and His ways.

Higher Power

Many Roman Catholics relate to the supernatural formally through Jesus Christ but practically through the mediation of Mary and the saints and in the context of ritual acts or ceremonies such as the "sacramentals" that may include blessed water or holy oil. Access to the supernatural, including miracles, visions, and the afterlife, is mediated by other channels than Christ alone and is often intertwined with superstitious practices. The gospel invites us to fear God alone, who is the Lord of all, and presents Jesus Christ as the only one who died, rose again, and is now seated at the right hand of the Father, interceding for us. Jesus has conquered death (1 Cor. 15:55–57) and has given us a spirit not of fear but of power, love, and sound judgment (2 Tim. 1:7).

Four Tips to Share the Gospel

Conversations never happen in a vacuum. This is why it is important to appreciate the different contexts in which we might find ourselves. Here are four tips that may be of some help in engaging Roman Catholics with the gospel. They are neither a four-step process nor a formula for success. They are rather lessons I have learned over the years in sharing the gospel with Roman Catholics.

Practical Tip #1: Don't assume or rely on common language.

Roman Catholics share much of our vocabulary, but they understand it differently. For example, words such as *salvation*, *the cross*, *sin*, and *grace* are all found in the Bible, but Roman Catholics don't understand them the same way. Salvation is thought of as an open-ended process, where our works and the merits we gain are necessary for it to be received. The cross is understood more as the Eucharist celebrated by the priest than as the once-and-for-all sacrifice of Jesus on Calvary. Sin is seen more as a sickness than spiritual death. We could go on and on. The point is that the same words have different meanings.

Moreover, there is often a gap between what the Roman Catholic Church teaches and what people who call themselves Catholics actually believe and do. The number of free-range Catholics, meaning people who are Catholics in their own way, is large and perhaps growing. We should not assume, just because someone says they are Catholic, that their beliefs are consistent with standard Catholic doctrine.

Instead of relying on an assumed common ground that is more rhetorical than real, let the Bible define your language and lead your conversation. Engage your Roman Catholic friends in Bible reading, Bible study, and Bible conversations as much as possible. Don't approach them with an "us versus them" attitude, but invite them to be exposed to Scripture and pray that the Holy Spirit will open their hearts.

As Catholics do open the Bible, they bring preconceived ideas about God's written Word that we should be aware of. For centuries, the Bible was thought of as being the book for experts (the priests) rather than the people. Catholics may fear the Bible as a dangerous book—remember that personal Bible reading was discouraged if not forbidden for Catholics until sixty years ago—and have skepticism about it absorbed from modern critical readings, as if it were an obscure book. Yet the Word of God is powerful to break through people's resistance. Plus, although portions of the Bible are read in the Mass, the average Catholic does not have a sense of the biblical flow of the gospel and the unity of Scripture as a single, yet composite book. Be sure to help your friend grasp the basic principles of biblical interpretation by showing the connections between the Old and New Testaments and how the gospel of Jesus Christ is the overarching message of the Bible.

How do we read the Bible and where do we start? Here are Mark Gilbert's suggestions that I also found helpful:[16]

- *Start simple.* Begin with one of the Gospels. Luke is good to start with, and so is Mark.

- *Read it as a book.* Help your friend to appreciate the gospel as one message grounded in history, rather than a bunch of isolated texts.
- *Listen to it.* In majority Catholic cultures, religion has been taught more by using symbols and pictures. Dealing with a text has not been the primary resource for catechism. Help your friend to reflect on the text of Scripture and to dig into it.
- *Ask questions.* Bible reading is a relatively new thing for most Catholics. Feel free to ask questions about what they understand and how the Word impacts them. Be ready to listen to them and don't quickly judge them. Help them to see the richness and depth of God's Word.
- *Do something about it.* God expects that as we get to know Him better in His Word, our lives will be impacted. So act on what you learn together with a prayer request, a course of action to commit to, or sharing with others what you have learned.

Practical Tip #2: Be prepared to wrestle with the exclusive nature of the gospel.

As you read or share Scripture together with your Catholic friends, all kinds of interesting conversations will come up. Usually, they will revolve around the sharp edges of the gospel.

For example, Roman Catholics may have a high respect for the Bible, but it's not their ultimate authority, so when confronted with something the Bible says that contradicts what their church teaches, they would rather question the authority of Scripture than the authority of the Roman Church. Moreover, Roman Catholics commend believing in Jesus, but faith in Christ is not sufficient to be saved; something more needs to be done by men and women. Roman Catholics often show a kind of love for Christ, but they rely on sub-mediators—Mary and the saints—who detract attention from Him and fill their devotional lives. In other words, what is at stake with them is acceptance of the Scripture alone, faith alone, and Christ alone principles of biblical faith.

Most Catholics would understand their spiritual conditions along these lines:

> I am basically a good person, certainly not perfect and with some failures, but I do my best to obey God's rules. There are so many rules that it is impossible to keep them, so confession is a way to deal with my failures. When I fail, then I try harder.

What is implied in this statement is a rejection of the exclusive claims of the gospel. The issue at stake is not a general belief in faith or grace, which are part of the Roman Catholic vocabulary. It is when faith is understood biblically as the only means to receive God's salvation and grace is understood biblically as the only ground to be saved that the problem will arise. Be sure to know to clearly present the "faith alone and grace alone" teaching of the gospel.

Practical Tip #3: Be ready to show the personal elements of the Christian life.

In reading the Bible together, make sure to share how the Bible impacts your life. In other words, combine biblical reading with your personal testimony. This step will be very helpful because it will encourage your friends to move beyond three obstacles.

1. *Beyond religion:* Nominal Roman Catholics tend to separate normal life from religion. Make sure you carefully show the impact of the Word on daily life, for example, in personal experience, work, church, and society. You can share your struggles and ongoing issues. The point is not to pretend to be perfect, but to show how the gospel impacts our lives.
2. *Beyond tradition:* Roman Catholics tend to see religion as a set of practices to be repeated as part of their cultural

identity. As Ray Galea rightly points out, "Catholicism is as much, or sometimes more, about belonging than believing."[17] Show the centrality of a relationship with Jesus, who is the Lord of the whole of life, and the importance of God's Word as the final authority in whatever we believe and do.

3. *Beyond the divide of the clergy/laity:* Many Catholics tend to consider religion a responsibility of the clergy that laypeople don't have. It is the clergy who mediates religion. Show instead that we are all responsible to nurture our Christian life in personal devotion and witness. The church is there to help us, not to replace personal responsibility.

One powerful resource in this respect is Timothy Keller's book, *The Prodigal God*.[18] The gospel parable in Luke 15 resonates with Catholics. They especially identify with the older brother's syndrome. In fact, the basis of the older brother's life can be summed up with a famous Latin expression: *do ut des,* or, "I give so that you may give." The reasoning of the older brother is as follows: "My Father, I strive to work for you, I fulfill my duty, I do what you ask so that one day you will give me the inheritance I deserve and to which I am entitled. I do all this to receive from you. I work to get in return. I give you one thing so that you may give me another thing."

All human religiosity, including Roman Catholic religiosity, is built around a distorted principle: I give to God so that He will give to me. Yet the Father loves His prodigal children. His inheritance is promised because they are His beloved children, not because of anything they must do. The prodigal God relates to us on the basis of His undeserved grace, on the basis of His love that led Him to give His only begotten Son, our Firstborn, to lay down His life for us.

One does not gain access to the Father's inheritance by merit: this is the false religion of the older brother, but it is not the will of the Father. The inheritance of salvation is received by grace on the basis of sonship. It is by grace alone. One becomes a son, therefore an heir, not because one deserves it, but because the Father adopts a penitent sinner to become His son. Once you become a child of God, you change your life and learn new ways. Yet it is not because we are good and faithful that we become heirs. It is because we are adopted as sons. To all who have received the Son, Jesus Christ, God has given the right to become children of God, that is, to those who believe in His name, who are born of God (John 1:12–13).

Practical Tip #4: Be prepared to integrate personal witness and church life.

Engaging in Bible reading and showing the power of the gospel in everyday life cannot be limited to our individual experiences only. Invite other Christian friends into the conversation to show how the gospel creates communities of followers of Jesus.

Remember that many disengaged Catholics continue to feel a sense of belonging to Mother Church without believing what she teaches or behaving in a way consonant with her moral code. The *Catechism* is still the official doctrinal reference point for Catholics, and all the requirements for being Catholics in good standing remain in place. However, the post–Vatican II tendency has been to dilute the traditional confessional expectations of the faithful and to instead invest in the expansion of the catholic embrace of all people, regardless of their confessional adherence to or coherence with the church's standards.

In other words, present-day Roman Catholicism is more "catholic" than "Roman," more interested in expanding the catholicity or inclusivity of the church, as envisaged at Vatican II, than in defending its doctrinal-institutional "Roman" markers, including the correspondence between professed faith in the Creed and the spiritual realities of daily life. One of the fundamental decisions made at Vatican II was to maximize the sacramental threshold of how one enters the church (baptism) and the sacramental condition of staying in the church (the Eucharist) rather than the confessional integrity of the faithful. As sociologist Luca Diotallevi has argued, it was the end of the "confessional religion" Roman Catholicism used to be since at least the Council of Trent.[19]

I've lived in Rome as an evangelical pastor and theologian for almost fifteen years. Most Catholic people I know attend Mass only on rare occasions and mumble the Creed when they attend, if they remember it. They have eclectic theologies and occasionally even more eclectic lifestyles. If at all retained in their memory, the Creed does not shape their belief system and life. For how many nominal Christians does the recitation of the Creed make a difference in their life? What does it mean to say "I believe . . ." for many people who, despite having been baptized and occasionally attending religious services, are not regenerated and, therefore, are not confessional believers in the biblical sense? They may recite the Creed, but this profession is often a rhetorical exercise with little spiritual value.

Believing and belonging go together. Roman Catholics tend to emphasize the latter at the expense of the former. Show the reality that the gospel forms a new community, the church. Invite them to church to see what a community of the gospel looks like. Connect them with your Christian friends and show them that you are not an isolated Christian but a member of a local church.

Furthermore, remember the importance of the ordinances instituted by Jesus Christ for the church, especially the Lord's Supper. Catholics are not used to listening as their primary way of receiving a message. Their religious mindset is shaped toward seeing and experiencing religion through other senses, such as sight, touch, and taste, all done in the context of community. Baptism and the Lord's Supper are the gospel made visible, and they impact Catholic imagination because they are visible signs. Invite your friend to a baptismal service. Your local church services are wonderful evangelistic tools to invite them to experience what it means for the gospel to be heard and seen.

Everyone's journey is different, so flexibility, adaptability, and patience must be practiced again and again. Moreover, every conversion to Christ is a miracle.[20] As you communicate the gospel to your Roman Catholic friends, pray that God will move in their hearts to open them to see the truth of the gospel and to respond to its message in obedience and faith.

Chapter 4

FAQs as We Witness

We have come to the last chapter of the book. After surveying the current reality of Roman Catholicism by defining it, addressing the crucial importance of personal conversion to Christ as the marker of biblical Christianity, and exploring ways and sharing tips to talk about Jesus with our Catholic friends, it is time to tackle some final, practical questions for gospel conversations. Hopefully, the answers given, while not exhaustive, will provide useful insights and food for thought.

Should We Pray with Catholics?

When I speak at conferences about Roman Catholicism and how evangelicals should relate to their Catholic friends, a question often arises: "What about joint prayer? Could or should evangelicals pray with Roman Catholics?" Let me offer my rules of thumb as I, too, wrestle with the issue.

1. The Bible is clear that we should pray for all men and women (e.g., 1 Tim. 2:1), so praying for friends, colleagues, and family members who are Roman Catholics is mandatory.

There is no doubt that praying for Roman Catholics is a God-given responsibility for all evangelicals.

2. The issue becomes more difficult when discussing praying *with* Roman Catholics. Praying with someone is a spiritual activity that presupposes the existence of spiritual bonds or fellowship in Christ. In other words, prayer with someone is legitimate when the people praying together are brothers and sisters in Christ, joining their hearts and voices to praise the triune God and intercede for various concerns in the name of Jesus Christ. Herein lies the problem: according to Roman Catholic doctrine, one becomes a Christian at baptism, normally received when a person is a newborn.[1] It is the sacrament of baptism that makes someone a Christian. This is what the *Catechism* says:

> Holy Baptism is the basis of the whole Christian life, the gateway to life in the Spirit (*vitae spiritualis ianua*), and the door which gives access to the other sacraments. Through Baptism we are freed from sin and reborn as sons of God; we become members of Christ, are incorporated into the Church and made sharers in her mission: "Baptism is the sacrament of regeneration through water in the word" (n. 1213).

In the evangelical faith, one becomes a Christian at conversion, when a person believes the gospel of Jesus Christ. The turning point is not the reception of a sacrament, the Roman Catholic view, but personal faith resulting in a transformed life, the biblical view. The reality is that a Roman

Catholic person might have received the sacrament of baptism but not be a believer in Christ, because she or he was never converted. If this is the case, she or he is not a sister or brother in Christ, and, therefore, there is no spiritual bond in Him, making it impossible to elevate our joint prayers to God. We can pray for her, we can of course pray with her, but we should pay attention not to imply that we are united in Christ if she is not a believer in the biblical sense. In my daily experience with my Roman Catholic neighbors, most were baptized by the Roman Catholic Church but show no evidence of a spiritual life as biblically understood. I cannot relate to them as spiritual brothers and sisters. While I gladly pray for them, I don't ask for their prayers, nor do I pray with them on the assumption that we are brothers and sisters in Christ.

3. Another reason common prayer is impossible is that Roman Catholicism believes in a different account of the gospel than the biblical one. There are some overlaps in language, but the basic truths of the gospel, such as the ultimate authority of the Bible in all matters of faith and life or salvation by faith alone, are fundamentally obscured in Catholicism. From different commitments arise contrasting appreciations of the gospel. For example, because Scripture is not the ultimate standard and we are thought of as contributing to our salvation through the merits of the saints, Roman Catholicism prescribes prayer to the saints and Mary as intercessors. These are not biblically warranted prayers. If you pray with a Roman Catholic, you may use similar words but express different faith commitments. It is better to avoid generating confusion and ambiguity and to respectfully

abstain from joint prayer if the people involved have not yet given signs of being converted to Christ. The fact that they are Roman Catholics does not necessarily mean they are brothers and sisters in the faith.

4. I don't deny that there are Roman Catholics who are genuinely converted. God's grace is at work in men and women who trust in Jesus Christ alone for their salvation and desire to follow the Word of God. However, these people have a problem with their Roman Catholic identity. If they follow Christ alone according to the Bible alone, they are inconsistent with their Roman Catholic faith. They may be believers in the biblical sense, but they are inconsistent Roman Catholics. While encouraging one another to grow in our faith, even if this means questioning Roman Catholic beliefs and practice, if a Roman Catholic is converted to Jesus Christ and not simply baptized, we can pray with them in informal and private settings.

5. I abstain from participating in joint prayer in public settings and events. Apart from the reasons above, particularly numbers 2 and 3, lies another consideration. Once you pray with someone in public, you have conveyed that all the participants share the same Christian faith and are brothers and sisters in Christ. Existing differences are but footnotes that do not impede fellowship. Because the Roman Catholic account of the gospel is flawed, if we participate in public joint prayer with Catholics, we accept as legitimate their version of the gospel, with only minor concerns over secondary issues—this is the symbolic message that comes across, at least. This message is even stronger when the people we pray with are Roman Catholic priests. If we pray in public

with them, we seem to recognize that the church they belong to and the account of the gospel it promotes are biblical expressions of the church and sufficiently faithful appreciations of the gospel. We must pay attention to the power of symbols. Ecumenical gatherings that include joint prayers often are intended to affirm that all participants recognize their respective communities as legitimate expressions of the biblical church.

6. In European ecumenical circles, many joint prayer events are organized during the Week of Prayer for Christian Unity, January 18–25, by the Roman Catholic Church and the World Council of Churches. Their view of the gospel and unity is based on the sacrament of baptism and not on personal conversion to Christ. The symbolic message that this initiative promotes is that all Christians, regardless of the denomination or tradition they belong to, are one, united as brothers and sisters. Since this is not the case, I don't participate in it. While I am willing to engage in dialogue with Roman Catholics at all levels, I consider joint prayer to be the privilege of born-again Christians, not representative members of different ecclesiastical bodies.

Can We Cooperate with the Roman Catholic Church?

In our global world, a cluster of questions confront evangelicals: Should we collaborate with Catholics? On which topics or areas? How far should we go? Is it possible to do mission together? Of course, much depends on the various contexts in which these questions are asked and those who are involved. For example, it is one thing to work with individual Catholics or lay groups; it is something else to join hands with the institutional Church of Rome. It is one thing to work together on areas of common concern in society, such as the promotion of Judeo-Christian values; it is something else altogether to engage in common mission and evangelism.

1. Alliance and Co-belligerence

When considering working together with Catholics, it may be useful to remember the lesson of twentieth-century evangelical apologist Francis Schaeffer (1912–84). Schaeffer was a Christian leader who introduced the expression "co-belligerence" to the present-day Christian vocabulary. In the midst of the cultural transitions of the seventies, he encouraged evangelicals to join with people of other religious persuasions for the sake of promoting specific concerns that were shared by a cross-section of society and that were under threat by secular tendencies, especially in the realm of basic moral values. Schaeffer's call to engage in the public square, working together with non-Christians, has been one of the motivating factors of recent evangelical involvement in society.

In suggesting a rationale for co-belligerence, Schaeffer made a distinction between forming alliances and engaging in co-belligerence. On the one hand, an alliance is a kind of unity based on truth, and, therefore, born-again Christians should restrict their alliances to those who receive Scripture as the standard of their lives. On the other hand, co-belligerence focuses on a specific issue and is open to all those who share a concern about it, whatever their backgrounds and motivating goals. Here is how Schaeffer defines it: "Co-belligerent is a *person with whom I do not agree on all sorts of vital issues, but who, for whatever reasons of their own, is on the same side in a fight for some specific issue of public justice.*"[2] Schaeffer believed this distinction between alliances and co-belligerence reflected biblical principles about unity among believers and cooperation with people of different faiths. Co-belligerence is not another way of talking about ecumenism. The latter has to do with the unity of believers according to the Bible; the former is related to possible cooperative efforts among people who do not share agreement on central truths of the gospel.

2. Biblical Foundations

The distinction between alliance and co-belligerence reflects the teaching of Scripture. Unity exists deep within the people of God on the basis of a common faith in Jesus Christ (Eph. 4:1–16). This unity allows alliances in terms of worship, prayer, evangelism, and gospel witness. This unity allows the church to follow the Great Commission all over the world, discipling the nations together (Matt. 28:16–20). This unity shows the power of the gospel to reconcile different people around the same Lord Jesus who sends His people forth to take the message of reconciliation to the world (2 Cor. 5:17–20). This unity is not what co-belligerence is about.

Scripture clearly distinguishes the unity of believers in Christ from other types of relationships without separating them. The Bible commands all men and women, Christians included, to inhabit the earth responsibly, taking care of the world and living peacefully with one another as much as possible. It also encourages the church to develop and maintain good relationships with their neighbors and to be committed to the good of others (Gen. 1:27–31; Jer. 29:5–7; Titus 3:1–2). In doing what the Bible requires, we will be in contact with different people who hold a plurality of worldviews and practice a variety of lifestyles. Our family members, coworkers, roommates, and friends may not be believers, yet we are called to live with them peaceably for the good of the community.

In one sense, co-belligerence is necessary, useful, and even inevitable. It is a task of our God-given humanity. It is part of our calling to live in this world without being of the world (John 17:14–18). For the Christian, neither total retreat nor self-imposed exclusion from the world is a viable option. The Christian life requires one to develop and nurture multiple networks of social relations. A mature faith can maintain relationships with different people without losing its Christian identity and gospel commitments. The important thing is to practice the distinction between alliance and co-belligerence.

3. Alliance or Co-belligerence?

Summarizing the questions I asked at the beginning, should evangelicals engage in alliances or acts of co-belligerence with Roman Catholics? Schaeffer encouraged co-belligerence with people of all persuasions, but he would limit alliances to Bible-believing, born-again Christians, therefore excluding the Church of Rome as an institution. The basic issue to address is whether or not the Catholic gospel held by the Church of Rome is the biblical gospel in its basic contours. The answer to this question leads to the answer of the previous one. If the answer is yes, the Roman Catholic gospel is the biblical gospel, then it follows that no theological restrictions should be put on alliances with Catholics. If the answer is no, the Roman Catholic gospel differs from the biblical gospel in significant ways, then we should practice careful discernment not to blur the distinction between collaborating on social issues and engaging in common mission. The former is possible; the latter isn't.

How Do We Debate with Catholics?

On June 20, 2023, in Naples, Italy, I had the privilege of debating my book, *Same Words, Different Worlds: Do Roman Catholics and Evangelicals Believe the Same Gospel?*, with a distinguished Roman Catholic theologian, Edoardo Scognamiglio, professor of dogmatic theology at the Pontifical Theological Faculty of Southern Italy. Scognamiglio is the author of several books in the areas of Christology, interreligious dialogue, and ecumenism.

Attended by about eighty people, the event was moderated well by a local pastor, and it was followed by questions and answers. Two different accounts of the gospel emerged in the conversation. The dialogue was conducted calmly and respectfully. I summarized the content of one of his books,[3] presenting a systematic analysis of Roman Catholic theology and practice and arguing that common use of words from the Bible does not mean that the evangelical and Roman Catholic faiths believe the same thing. The words *church*, *grace, forgiveness, mercy, justification, evangelization,* and *mission* are given different meanings, because Rome is not committed to Scripture alone. Instead, the Catholic Church blends the Bible with her own traditions, ultimately resulting in a different version of the gospel.

Scognamiglio proved to be a serious scholar. His reading of my book was appreciative and positive. He also reiterated that contemporary Roman Catholicism wants to be open to evangelicals, as well as everybody else, but it is not really interested in a journey of biblical reformation. From Scognamiglio's words, one could observe a conciliatory attitude, not one of hostility as was the case in the past, at least in Italy. After all, according to his view, shaped by Vatican II and its ecumenical outlook, we are all Christians, all children of God. It emerged that Roman Catholicism is the religion of the both/and, according to which different versions of the Christian faith are complementary, while Roman Catholicism in its estimation enjoys the fullness of that faith.

Scognamiglio acknowledged not all Roman Catholics are disciples of Christ, but how can this statement be reconciled with the Roman Catholic dogma of baptism being the sacrament that takes away original sin and regenerates the recipient? He also admitted popular devotions, such as the veneration of the liquifiable "blood" of Saint Januarius, famous in Naples, could be deviant, but how can this admission be reconciled with official Roman Catholic approval of practices contrary to Scripture?

The public conversation with Professor Scognamiglio was a useful exercise in dialogue. The importance of publicly debating the faith needs to be underlined. Jesus debated the scribes, Paul reasoned with the philosophers, Irenaeus wrote against heretics, Luther confronted Cajetan, Calvin replied to Sadoleto, and we could go on and on. The biblical faith is not afraid of publicly engaging other viewpoints.

After presenting my aforementioned book in the context of debates with Roman Catholic theologians, I gathered three lessons for public dialogue. I hope they are useful in everyday conversations as well, both within and beyond the European context.

1. Question the "mystique" of ecumenical unity

Present-day Roman Catholic theologians are children of Vatican II and have absorbed its pro-ecumenical theology. They generally have a neutral-to-positive view of Protestant theology, often equating it with liberal, post-liberal, or Barthian theology, while showing little acquaintance with evangelical theology for which they don't have categories. They tend to praise the good things they perceive in Protestantism, such as a tradition of accessibility to the Bible and personal responsibility in ethics. In their studies, they have been taught that the Ecumenical century, meaning the twentieth century, overcame the division between Rome and the Reformation. The ecumenical narrative tells them that, with Vatican II, the Roman Church has absorbed the positive elements of the Reformation, engrafting them into the Roman Catholic tradition. The Reformation is over in their view; today is the time for unity. This kind of "mantra" can be addressed counterculturally.

In engaging with Roman Catholic thinkers, one must be aware of where they come from and be prepared to offer a different account. The evangelical must present a counter-narrative whereby the Reformation is not over, given the fact that, despite the common language used by evangelicals and Catholics, the issues that surfaced during the Reformation are still with us. Rome rejected the supreme authority of the Bible and salvation by faith alone, and it still rejects them. The 2016 document "Is the Reformation Over?", signed by hundreds of evangelical leaders worldwide, is useful in highlighting these ongoing divisions.[4]

2. Maintain apologetic intentionality

Because of their ecumenical attitude, Roman Catholic theologians have little desire to engage in meaningful apologetics. In their view, the Council of Trent, which anathematized the Reformation, belongs to the past, and its condemnations against Protestants need to be read in light of the positive view of non-Catholic Christians at Vatican II. Doing "controversialist" theology, such as arguing for Roman Catholic positions against Protestant ones, is something they generally dislike and don't want to do. Instead, they want to bring together different perspectives and look for what is good in each, without critically analyzing what is wrong. Seeking catholicity of doctrine and practice, embracing diversity into unity, is what they prefer. They don't want to do apologetics; they want to do ecumenism.

I have always felt responsible for maintaining an apologetic edge in my conversations with Roman Catholic theologians. The risk of losing it and transforming the dialogue into a celebration of our alleged unity is real. Without being emotionally antagonistic, it is the task of the evangelical theologian to raise the critical issues, including the authority of Scripture, the exclusivity of Christ, the necessity of conversion, and the call to abandon idolatry, and to argue that Roman Catholicism runs counter to biblical Christianity on several fundamental points. That is perhaps not a nice thing to say, but it is necessary for the gospel's sake. Apologetics is the privilege and the responsibility of all Christians.

3. Focus on gospel issues

Dialogue with a Roman Catholic theologian is an intellectual feast. Generally, you are dealing with a sophisticated academic who is an expert on many topics. However, there is a risk the conversation may become a sterile exercise, just two or more experts talking to one another, losing the gospel focus that healthy theology must always have. There is also a danger of sidetracking the dialogue into obscure disputes over historical and doctrinal details. If the conversation moves to peripheral issues or becomes polemical over secondary elements, we must bring it back to the gospel. The gospel must always be at the center. As I meet with Roman Catholic theologians, my first commitment is not to be a public defender of the evangelical movement but to be a gospel ambassador. One time, while debating about my book with a lay theologian in Sicily, she commented on the wrongs done by Protestants across the ages. I said, "I agree with you. We have made many mistakes, and we must apologize for them. This is why we need the gospel." Then I went back to talking about the good news of Jesus.

The important differences between Roman Catholicism and the evangelical faith in no way invalidated the usefulness and importance of dialogue. While maintaining a clear identity, one should not avoid encountering other faith communities to share, defend, and commend the gospel. The gospel must be proclaimed to all respectfully, persuasively, and competently. The underlying conviction of the Christian is that the truth is powerful, and the Holy Spirit uses it to regenerate hearts and minds. The Lord has promised His Word never returns empty.

What about Our Similarities and Differences?

Born-again believers and Catholics share apparent similarities in the language they use (e.g., gospel, God, salvation) and in some practices that influence their lives (e.g., prayer). At the same time, significant differences stand between them. Taking into account both proximities and distances, here is a list of questions that may be asked by our Catholic friends in gospel conversations.

1. What are the similarities between Catholicism and the evangelical faith?

The language between the two faiths is similar, but the meanings are different. We speak of "grace," but for Catholicism, it is a force that is infused through the sacraments; in the gospel message, it is God who gives himself in Christ through the Spirit. Rome confuses justification and sanctification, whereas in the Bible, justification is the righteousness of Christ imputed to the sinner by faith alone from which the path of sanctification is born. The Bible is the same, apart from the Deuterocanonical books of the Old Testament, but the way we receive, interpret, and respond to Scripture is different. The common language about the triunity of God and the divinity of Jesus Christ may seem to be the same. However, given the differences in all doctrinal and practical areas, there is no deep commonality even in Trinitarian and Christological doctrines. The apparent similarity is more formal than real.

2. What are the main points of difference?

The Word of God is a crucial difference. For Rome, the Bible is part of the Word of God, along with tradition and the magisterium; for the evangelical faith, Scripture is the written, inspired, and authoritative Word of God that truthfully attests to the incarnate Word of God: Jesus Christ. The Reformation's doctrine of *sola Scriptura* sums this up. Another crucial point of difference concerns salvation. For the evangelical faith, we are saved through Christ alone by faith alone. For Rome, the mediation of the sacraments and the role of our works are central. Although there are many differences between the Roman Catholic and the evangelical faith at various levels, including Mariology, the church, and devotional practices, the differences are all interconnected and, in the last analysis, stem from a radically divergent basic orientation that informs all doctrines and practices. This divergence cannot be explained in psychological, historical, or cultural terms, nor does it derive from different doctrinal emphases that could somehow be made complementary in the catholic synthesis. The divergence stems from core commitments about the Bible and salvation and spreads out into all other areas.

3. Do we believe in Mary?

For Bible-believing Christians, Mariology is a source of puzzlement. We love Mary, but we cannot come to terms with what happened to the memory of the young lady called by God the Father to be the bearer of the Lord Jesus. We don't see how the biblical Mary can be reconciled with the hypertrophic Mary of subsequent Mariology. It seems to rely on rules and criteria that go far beyond what is written in the Bible. Roman Catholic Mariology, as it stands currently, must go through a process of radically biblical deconstruction if it wants to become a biblically defined and viable Christian option. All the stratified accumulation of Marian suggestions, expansions, and developments should go through the healthy refinement of clear biblical teaching in order to be given scriptural shape. Pointing our attention to the Son, the Lord Jesus Christ—this was Mary's true way.[5]

4. Do we not agree on the Trinity?

One common refrain in ecumenical discourse is that all historic religious traditions—Roman Catholicism, Eastern Orthodoxy, and various branches of Protestantism—differ in the way they understand salvation and the nature and role of the church and the sacraments, but they agree on the Christian doctrines of the Trinity and Christology. While this is formally true at one level, a more profound and closer look reveals cracks in this widespread assumption. The contrast between Catholicism and evangelicalism is more evident and sharper in the areas of salvation and the church, yet these areas are inextricably related to Trinitarian doctrine as the core of Christian theology. Against this background, the alleged consensus on the Trinitarian framework of the Christian faith appears more limited than often thought. Moreover, developments within the Catholic Church during the centuries following the early church's clarification of the doctrines of the Trinity and Christology indicate that this adherence may be more formal than substantial.[6] How the Trinitarian framework is received, believed, and applied indicates *a significant* distance between the two traditions despite formal points of agreement. The words used are the same, but the theological worlds they open are different.

5. Are we not all Christians?

The widespread assumption in today's world is that biblical Christianity embraces all those who identify as Christians, whether they be Roman Catholics, Protestants, Eastern Orthodox, or something else. The Bible, however, teaches that Christians are disciples of Christ, those who are born again and converted. Conversion points to a time when we were not converted and a time when we became converted and believed, turning away from our idols and being forgiven of our sins. According to Roman Catholicism, regeneration happens at baptism, and conversion is an ongoing process instead of a once-and-for-all experience. We stand in permanent need of being converted, and that fits the sacramental Roman Catholic view of the Christian life, whereby we depend on the sacraments of the church from beginning to end. Catholics and evangelicals use the same word, *Christian*, but mean different things. Therefore, we need to underline the cruciality of biblical conversion. Being labeled a Christian because of a received sacrament or because one belongs to a Christian family or culture does not make anyone a disciple of Christ. The message of the gospel must be proclaimed to everyone, and many Catholics do not know what the gospel is; it is an act of love and a Christian duty to engage in gospel conversations with them. The gospel must be shared with love. Our attitude must be patient, understanding, attentive, but also challenging. Then, if a Catholic reads the Bible and believes in Christ, idols must be abandoned.

6. What about justification? Isn't that issue resolved?

Five hundred years ago, much discussion took place on justification by faith. Is faith sufficient to be justified, as the Reformers argued, or is faith only necessary but not sufficient, as the Council of Trent rebutted? Many people have rightly given attention to the 1999 "Joint Declaration on the Doctrine of Justification" (JDDJ) signed by the Roman Catholic Church and the World Lutheran Federation. They think the disagreement is now resolved. In the JDDJ, the Catholic Church uses the language of "grace alone" (n. 15) and applies it to justification. Taken out of context, the phrase would make sense from an evangelical perspective. Yet it must be understood in relation to the whole document of the JDDJ. For the Catholic Church, "by grace alone" means that grace is intrinsically, constitutionally, and necessarily linked to the sacraments and, thus, to the church that administers it and the works implemented by it. Salvation, therefore, cannot be by grace alone through faith alone. In JDDJ there is an attempt to redescribe this theological understanding of salvation in language that appears biblical. However, the new description does not change the theology of the Council of Trent, according to which grace is sacramental and experienced inside of an open-ended process of salvation, rather than being grounded on a declaration of God based on the righteousness of Christ, a synergistic dynamic of the process of salvation. JDDJ's understanding of grace appears to remain aligned with the Catholic heritage of the Council of Trent, in an updated form, rather than with classic Protestant theology. In this sense, JDDJ is a clear exercise in increased catholicity on the part of Rome, demonstrating its ability to absorb ideas without changing its core. Roman Catholicism has not become more evangelical in the biblical sense. The chasm on justification by faith separating Rome and the Protestant faith remains.[7]

7. Is it possible to be a born-again believer in the Catholic Church?

It can be the case that your Catholic friends or neighbors show signs of true regeneration and authentic devotion to Christ, yet they attend the Catholic church, continuing to receive the sacraments and participating at religious festivals. They seem to love Christ and trust Him alone for their salvation. What to do in these cases? First of all, let's rejoice that God's grace is at work everywhere. It is not our church affiliation that saves us, but Christ alone by faith alone. What matters is to be a born-again believer. There is another side of the coin, though. As the Italian Evangelical Alliance's document argues:

> God's grace is at work in men and women who, although they may consider themselves Catholics, trust in God alone, and seek to develop a personal relationship with him, read the Scriptures and lead a Christian life. These people, however, must be encouraged to think through the issue of whether their faith is compatible with membership of the Catholic Church. They must be helped to examine critically residual Catholic elements in their thinking in the light of God's Word (n. 12).[8]

While Catholic people may show signs of regeneration and, therefore, be true believers, the Roman Catholic Church is not the best place or context for biblical discipleship and growth to occur. Its belief system is biblically flawed and obfuscates the gospel at best. Its practices are often characterized by spiritual compromise and deviations (e.g., veneration of Mary, indulgences, Eucharistic adoration). Its institutional setting resembles that of an empire rather than what the biblical church should look like. Its core commitments are not shaped around Scripture alone as the supreme authority. This is to say that, sooner or later, a born-again Christian still identifying as Catholic must come to terms with distancing herself from the Roman Catholic Church and becoming part of a Bible-believing, Christ-centered, evangelical church. It may take time and be a long and perhaps painful process, but this outcome cannot be overlooked. The gospel compels us to follow Christ and to obey His Word. The Roman Catholic Church is hardly the place where this can happen on a long-term basis and with spiritually fruitful results.

Appendix 1

Christ Alone: A Sermon for All, Especially Our Catholic Friends[1]

Bible Readings: Isaiah 53:1–12; 1 John 2:1–2

The word *Christian* has Christ at its center. A Christian is a follower of Christ. The name was given in the city of Antioch when the community of Jesus's disciples began to consolidate outside the borders of Judea (Acts 11:26). The need arose to name these people, and the term *Christian* was given. It is evident, then, that Christianity has the person and work of Jesus Christ in its DNA. Yet in the sixteenth century, it became necessary to return to that definition because the reference to Christ had become generic and confusing. The Protestant Reformation insisted on the expression "Christ alone." The centrality of Jesus Christ was threatened, and the focus on Jesus had become blurred. It was necessary to put the person of Jesus back in the only place worthy of Him: the center.

Today many people call themselves Christians because they have a remote connection to a faded image of Christ. It's a name that can say little, almost nothing. Perhaps you are in this situation. You were born into a Christian family, you've had this name stuck to you since you were a child, but beyond some small emotion that it stirs, the name doesn't say much about you, and it is distant from your life. Today you need to hear what "Christ alone" means. You see, after all, the issues of five hundred years ago are not that distant from today. So many people refer to Christ and call themselves Christians, but what Christ and what Christianity are they talking about?

Unique in His Person

Questions about Christ are not new. In one episode in His life, Jesus asked His friends, "Who do people say that the Son of Man is?" (Matt. 16:13). Jesus's identity has always caused discussion among His followers. However, Jesus also asked, "But you . . . who do you say that I am?" (v. 15). To talk about Jesus is not to do so in the abstract or in general terms, as if it were about what others think. Jesus wants to make the question personal and engaging. It is as if He said, "It is not enough for Me to know what others say, but I want to know what *you* think of Me." What do you think about Jesus? This is the point that really interests Him.

Right away, following Jesus's life, death, and resurrection, the church realized it was dealing with a unique person. Jesus is a unique person. On the one hand, He was and is God, truly God, fully God. In claiming to be the Son of God, one with the Father, and from the beginning with God, Jesus had to be recognized as God Himself. His powerful works—miracles, healings, and His resurrection from the dead—showed that divine omnipotence was at work in Him. Jesus is not just a semi-god, not just a prophet, not just an inspired prophet even, but God. This was clear from the beginning.

On the other hand, Jesus had been a man, truly a man, fully man. He was born, had a body, ate, slept, washed, wept, and walked. He could be touched to ascertain that He had a flesh-and-blood body. He was not a ghost, not an apparition, but a real person. True God on the one hand; true man on the other—born, raised, died, resurrected, and ascended to heaven.

Herein lies the uniqueness of His person. There has never existed nor will there ever be another equal to Him. He is God who speaks to us about God, acts as God, and moves as God. He was a man in order to identify Himself with us and to act on our behalf. Only Christ has done that. Among all the religious figures of the world found in the Pantheon or in the temples of the Roman Forum, among all the prophets of the world religions, among all the heroes of the cultures of the earth, Jesus is the only one who summed up in His person divinity and humanity—the full being of God and the full being of man. He is the Word made flesh (John 1:14). He is the Son of God who came to save the world. The church immediately had to come to terms with the uniqueness of His divine and human person.

Christ would become the center of the gospel message to be radiated to the whole world. In obedience to the message of the Bible and in continuity with the early church, five hundred years ago, Luther and the Protestant Reformation reaffirmed Christ's centrality. Only Christ had been man and God at the same time. Maybe this is not language you are familiar with, or maybe you don't think it makes a difference in your life. Are you sure? Isn't His person worth paying attention to?

Unique in His Work

What was at the center of the Reformation five hundred years ago was another cornerstone of the biblical message. Only Christ is God-man in a living person, so only Christ is the Mediator between God and man. As God-man, there is no one other than He who can lead us, guide us, and bring us to God!

This was a teaching that was obscured at the time. Along with Christ or as an alternative to Christ, Christians had turned to saints to receive grace and blessings. Saints were heroic figures in Christian history who were attributed with the ability to mediate, that is, to be intermediaries between God and the faithful. Thanks to their heroic lives, they had earned recognition as mediators and were recommended to the faithful to rely on them to obtain grace. In addition to the saints, the figure of Mary as mediatrix had acquired a prominent place in the medieval church. Not the Mary who is presented in the Bible, the mother of Jesus, a special person, certainly, but like the rest of us sinful men and women. In the lives of so many who did not read the Bible but relied on their devotions, Mary had been inflated to the point of becoming another mediator, a mother who dispenses God's grace to her children. Instead of turning only to Christ, true man and true God, many devoted themselves to an abnormal

APPENDIX 1: CHRIST ALONE

and inflated understanding of Mary, thinking that she would protect and bless their lives.

The Reformation was intended to be a strong, prophetic call to the church. Warning: the Christian life professes that Jesus is man *and* God and relies on Jesus as the only mediator between God and the world. If Jesus was truly man, who gave His life for us and rose from the dead, why rely on the saints who can do nothing for us and, moreover, died and were buried like everyone else? If Jesus was truly God who became flesh to be the way, the truth, and the life, why rely on Mary who is a creature like all others and who, as exemplary as her life was, can do nothing for us since she died like everyone else? Why seek the mediation of others if Jesus was the only God-man and is the only mediator?

In St. Peter's Square there is a powerful illustration of the religiosity that the gospel wants to bring biblical reformation to. There in the square, on Bernini's colonnade, there are dozens of statues of saints standing halfway between the people and the sky. Those statues represent the visible saints to whom people can turn. God is invisible, but the saints are visible. God is far away, but the saints are near. Do you understand what is at stake here? What about Christ? What about the cross of Christ? What about the uniqueness of His person and work? Only Christ is the Savior, and He alone is the mediator. He alone is the person by whom we can be saved. The Bible says we are to imitate the faith of those who have lived for God (Heb. 13:7), but it never, ever says to turn to them as mediators. They can do nothing for us, because they have done nothing for our salvation. They too, like us, depend in all things on Christ alone. Jesus alone as God and man gave His life so that those who believe in Him will not perish but have eternal life.

Unique in Your Life?

"Christ alone" is a cornerstone of the Christian faith. Today many people challenge its uniqueness in two ways. First, by believing in ourselves to be our own god. We can think we are the absolute holders of our lives and that we are divine. Instead of recognizing only Christ as God-man, many believe they are their own god. Not "Christ alone" but "me alone" is the religion of our time. Are you among the adherents of this religion? Do you think you are the god of yourself? Know that it is a deception, a deadly lie. You will not save yourself, and your illusions of making it on your own will soon give way to the tragic reality of death. Only in Christ, God made man, is there salvation for those who believe.

The second way in which "Christ alone" is challenged is through the addition of human mediators to the only mediator we have. Instead of having Christ as the only mediator, many seek other pseudo-mediators, thinking them closer and more at hand. In Italy, most people who call themselves religious are, in fact, devotees of other figures who distract from Christ and deflect their faith from being based on Christ alone. In Rome, these two alternatives to the centrality of Christ are most powerful: many people think they are their own god or rely on other mediators. Are you among them?

Five hundred years ago, the Reformation called everyone back to the Bible as the supreme authority for life and called everyone to believe in Christ alone to be saved. Now the Christian faith stands or falls on what Martin Luther wrote in his 1529 *Small Catechism*:

> I believe that Jesus Christ, true God, begotten of the Father in eternity, and also a true human being, born of the virgin Mary, is my Lord. He has redeemed me, a lost and condemned human being. He has purchased and freed me from all sins, from death, and from the power of the devil, not with gold or silver but with his holy, precious blood and with his innocent suffering and death. He has done all this in order that I may belong to him, live under him in his kingdom, and serve him in eternal righteousness, innocence, and blessedness, just as he is risen from the dead and lives and rules eternally. This is most certainly true.[2]

Amen. Can you say it for yourself?

Appendix 2

Helpful Resources

Website

Two Ways to Live
https://twowaystolive.com/

> Not specifically designed for Catholics, but very relevant for gospel conversations with Catholics.

Courses

Mark Gilbert, *The God Who Saves* (Kingsford: Matthias Media, 2006).

> Five Bible studies for people like sincere Catholics who think that faith matters.

Timothy Keller, *The Prodigal God: Recovering the Heart of the Christian Faith* (London: John Murray Press, 2009), with study guide.

> Jesus reveals God's prodigal grace toward both the irreligious and the moralistic. This

> book will challenge both the devout Catholic and skeptical Catholic to see Christianity in a whole new way.

Hope Explored
https://www.christianityexplored.org/courses/hope-explored/

> Over three sessions, *Hope Explored* presents the life, death, and resurrection of Jesus and provides an opportunity to discover how He fulfills three great longings we all experience: the longings for hope, peace, and purpose.

Videos

Talking with Catholics about Jesus
Mark Gilbert, Simon Cowell, Chris Overhall
https://matthiasmedia.com.au/products/talking-with-catholics-about-jesus

> This video and workbook course is an opportunity for small groups and individuals to better understand their Catholic relatives, friends, and neighbors and have great conversations with them about Jesus.

Truth Unites
Gavin Ortlund
https://truthunites.org/videos/

> Truth Unites offers resources in church history, theology, philosophy, and apologetics, many of which are helpful resources for conversations with Catholics.

Notes

Introduction

1. They are real people, but personal names have been changed.

Chapter 1

1. For a summary: https://www.sbts.edu/news/in-presidential-address-mohler-outlines-four-temptations-facing-the-evangelical-theological-society/ (accessed June 26, 2024).

2. See my articles "Christian Unity vis-à-vis Roman Catholicism: A Critique of the Evangelicals and Catholics Together Dialogue," *Evangelical Review of Theology* 27, no. 4 (2003): 337–52; and "Evangelicals and Catholics Together (1994–2015)," *Vatican Files* (March 9, 2015), https://vaticanfiles.org/en/2015/03/103-evangelicals-and-catholics-together-1994-2015/ (accessed June 26, 2024).

3. George Weigel, *Evangelical Catholicism: Deep Reform in the 21st-Century Church* (New York: Basic Books, 2013). See my critique, Leonardo De Chirico, *Same Words, Different Worlds: Do Roman Catholics and Evangelicals Believe the Same Gospel?* (London: IVP, 2021), 24–27.

4. English edition: Karl Adam, *The Spirit of Catholicism*, trans. Dom J. McCann (New York: Macmillan, 1929).

5. Romano Guardini, *Vom Wesen katholischer Weltanschauung* (Basel: Hess, 1953).

6. English edition: Henri De Lubac, *Catholicism: Christ and the Common Destiny of Man*, trans. Lancelot C. Sheppard – Sister Elizabeth Englund (San Francisco: Ignatius Press, 1988).

7. English edition: Hans Urs von Balthasar, *In the Fullness of Faith: On the Centrality of the Distinctively Catholic*, trans. E. T. Oakes (San Francisco: Ignatius Press, 1988).

8. English edition: Walter Kasper, *The Catholic Church: Nature, Reality and Mission*, trans. Thomas Hoebel (Edinburgh: Bloomsbury, 2015).

9. For useful presentations of Roman Catholic doctrines and practices from a Protestant perspective, see Ray Galea, *Nothing in My Hand I Bring: Understanding the Differences between Roman Catholic and Protestant Beliefs* (Kingsford: Matthias Media, 2007); Norman Geisler and Ralph MacKenzie, *Roman Catholics and Evangelicals: Agreements and Differences* (Grand Rapids, MI: Baker Books, 1995); R. C. Sproul, *Are We Together? A Protestant Analyzes Roman Catholicism* (Sanford, FL: Reformation Trust, 2012); Gregg R. Allison, *40 Questions about Roman Catholicism* (Grand Rapids, MI: Kregel, 2021).

10. The text can be found in *Biblioteca della Riforma italiana*, ed. Enrico Comba (Firenze: Claudiana, 1883), 81.

11. More on this in my *A Christian Pocket Guide to the Papacy: Its Origin and Role in the 21st Century* (Fearn: Christian Focus, 2015).

12. *Catechism of the Catholic Church* (1992), n. 882, https://www.vatican.va/archive/ENG0015/__P2A.HTM (accessed August 6, 2024).

13. *Catechism of the Catholic Church* (1992), n. 937, https://www.vatican.va/archive/ENG0015/__P2A.HTM (accessed August 6, 2024).

14. Gregg R. Allison, *Roman Catholic Theology and Practice: An Evangelical Assessment* (Wheaton, IL: Crossway, 2014), 42–67.

15. Joseph McLelland, *The Visible Words of God: An Exposition of the Sacramental Theology of Peter Martyr Vermigli, A. D. 1500–1562* (Edinburgh: Oliver and Boyd, 1957).

16. Vittorio Subilia, *La nuova cattolicità del cattolicesimo* (Torino: Claudiana, 1967).

17. Italian Evangelical Alliance, "An Evangelical Approach Towards Understanding Roman Catholicism," *European Journal of Theology* X (2001): 32–35.

NOTES

18. Italian Evangelical Alliance, "An Evangelical Approach Towards Understanding Roman Catholicism."

Chapter 2

1. This section is a summary of my article "To Be or Not to Be: Exercising Theological Stewardship of the Name Christian," *Foundations: An International Journal of Evangelical Theology*, No. 82 (Spring 2022): 8–22.

2. John Stott rightly argues that "Luke has so far referred to them as 'disciples' (6:1), 'saints' (9:13), 'brothers and sisters' and 'brothers' (1:16; 9:30), 'believers' (10:45), those 'who were being saved' (2:47) and the people 'who belonged to the Way' (9:2)." See John R. W. Stott, *The Message of Acts* (Leicester: IVP, 1990), 205.

3. James I. Packer, *I Want to Be a Christian* (Wheaton, IL: Tyndale House, 1977), 140.

4. See "The Lausanne Covenant" (1974), in J. D. Douglas, ed., *Let the Earth Hear His Voice. A Comprehensive Reference Volume on World Evangelization* (Minneapolis, MN: World Wide Publisher, 1975), 4, https://lausanne.org/statement/lausanne-covenant#cov (accessed August 6, 2024).

5. John Stott, *Christ the Controversialist: The Basics of Belief* (Leicester: IVP, 1970, 1996), 109–10.

6. On the *hapax* and *mallon* as defining categories for evangelical theology, see John Stott, *Evangelical Truth: A Personal Plea for Unity* (Leicester: Inter-Varsity Press, 1999).

7. *Christian Witness to Nominal Christians Among Roman Catholics* (Lausanne Occasional Papers 10, 1980), https://www.lausanne.org/content/lop/lop-10 (accessed June 26, 2024).

8. Here I use material already presented in my article "Salvation Belongs to the Lord: Evangelical Consensus in Dialogue with Roman Catholicism," *Evangelical Review of Theology* 39, no. 4 (2015): 292–310.

9. D. W. Bebbington, *Evangelicalism in Modern Britain: A History from 1730s to the 1980s* (London: Unwin Hyman, 1989). On Bebbington's overall understanding of Evangelicalism, see the recent and helpful

critical discussion in Michael A. G. Haykin and Kenneth J. Stewart, eds., *The Emergence of Evangelicalism: Exploring Historical Continuities* (Nottingham: Apollos, 2008).

10. Stott, *Christ the Controversialist*, 33. In the same book, Stott argues that evangelical Christianity is "theological," "biblical," "original," and "fundamental," 27–46.

11. There is a recent study on being "born again" by John Piper, *Finally Alive: What Happens When We Are Born Again* (Fearn: Christian Focus, 2010).

12. Stephen R. Holmes, "Evangelical Doctrine: Basis for Unity or Cause of Division?", *Scottish Bulletin of Evangelical Theology* 30, no. 1 (2012): 64.

13. Klaas Runia, "What Is Evangelical Theology?", *Evangelical Review of Theology* 21, no. 4 (1997): 299. See also David Wells, *Turning to God: Biblical Conversion in the Modern World* (Exeter: Paternoster, 1989).

14. John Newton, "Amazing Grace," public domain.

15. James I. Packer and Thomas C. Oden, *One Faith: The Evangelical Consensus* (Downers Grove, IL: IVP, 2004), 160.

16. It should be noted that the worldview of the "sinner's prayer" is a topic of growing uneasiness in evangelical circles. It is deemed to be too simplistic, too individualistic, too modernistic, too superficial, too close to Western cultural patterns of individual decision-making processes and far from other cultural patterns, etc. Having said all this and being aware of its weaknesses—see *Christianity Today* 2012 September editorial, http://www.christianitytoday.com/ct/2012/september/the-evangelical-jesus-prayer.html (accessed June 27, 2024)—the "sinner's prayer" is a "monument" of present-day evangelical spirituality that needs to be grappled with.

17. This aspect is well presented in the 1996 World Evangelical Fellowship document on Roman Catholicism: Paul Schrotenboer, ed., *Roman Catholicism: A Contemporary Evangelical Perspective* (Grand Rapids, MI: Baker, 1987), par. 8.

18. Henri Blocher, "The Nature of Biblical Unity," in J. D. Douglas, ed., *Let the Earth Hear His Voice*, 390. Here Blocher is talking about the

sacrament of baptism, but his argument can be extended to the sacraments as a whole.

19. Stott, *Christ the Controversialist*, 120–21.

20. See my *Same Words, Different Worlds: Do Roman Catholics and Evangelicals Believe the Same Gospel?* (London: IVP, 2021), 38–45.

21. Stott, *Evangelical Truth*, 34–38. I have applied this distinction in assessing the Roman Catholic language of "prolongation" of the Incarnation, "representation" of the Eucharist, and the "dynamic" time of Revelation; see "The Blurring of Time Distinctions in Roman Catholicism," *Themelios* 29, no. 2 (2004): 40–46.

22. For an introductory discussion on the different theologies of universalism, see James I. Packer, "Evangelicals and the Way of Salvation," in K. S. Kantzer and C. F. H. Henry, eds., *Evangelical Affirmations* (Grand Rapids, MI: Zondervan, 1990), 107–36.

23. Karl Rahner, *Theological Investigations*, vol. 6, trans. Karl and Boniface Kruger (Baltimore: Helicon, 1969), 395.

24. *Karl Rahner in Dialogue: Conversations and Interviews, 1965–1982*, P. Imhof and H. Biallowons, eds. (New York: Crossroads, 1986), 207.

25. As it is rightly argued by Pietro Bolognesi, "Catholicisme romain et protestantisme évangélique: réconciliation, mais sous quelles conditions?", *La Revue Réformée* N. 263 (2012/4).

26. "The Lausanne Covenant" (1974) in J. D. Douglas, ed., *Let the Earth Hear His Voice: A Comprehensive Reference Volume on World Evangelization*, 4. See also https://lausanne.org/statement/lausanne-covenant#cov (accessed August 6, 2024).

27. "The Lausanne Covenant," 6.

28. See https://isthereformationover.com/ in various languages (accessed June 26, 2024). For a thoughtful presentation of the theological significance and ongoing relevance of the five "solus, sola" of the Reformation, see Kevin J. Vanhoozer, *Biblical Authority after Babel: Retrieving the Solas in the Spirit of Mere Protestant Christianity* (Grand Rapids, MI: Brazos, 2016).

Chapter 3

1. Timothy Keller, *Center Church: Doing Balanced, Gospel-Centered Ministry in Your City* (Grand Rapids, MI: Zondervan, 2012), 89.
2. Keller, *Center Church*, 90.
3. Chris Castaldo, *Talking with Catholics about the Gospel: A Guide for Evangelicals* (Grand Rapids, MI: Zondervan, 2015).
4. I have to say that I find it difficult to accept the "evangelical Catholics" category. For me it is an oxymoron. Castaldo rightly defines evangelicalism in theological terms by referring to the 1974 "Lausanne Covenant" as a representative evangelical document. Lausanne highlights the authority of Scripture, the uniqueness of Jesus Christ, salvation by grace alone through faith alone, the need for conversion, and the commitment to evangelism and mission. If this is the meaning of evangelical (and I fully agree with it), then this "evangelical Catholic" category falls apart. According to this meaning of evangelical, you are either an evangelical or a Roman Catholic. You cannot be both.
5. Ray Galea, *Nothing in My Hand I Bring: Understanding the Difference between Catholic and Protestant Beliefs* (Kingsford: Matthias Media, 2007), 24–27.
6. In another book, Castaldo gives helpful tips on how to do it. Among them: "Don't be a pit bull," "Don't attempt to debate people into the kingdom," "Be cautious of emotional intensity," "Keep the main thing the main thing," Chris Castaldo, *Holy Ground: Walking with Jesus as a Former Catholic* (Grand Rapids, MI: Zondervan, 2009), 172–82.
7. Gregg R. Allison, *40 Questions about Roman Catholicism* (Grand Rapids, MI: Kregel, 2021), 321.
8. Castaldo, *Talking with Catholics about the Gospel*, 87.
9. Keller, *Center Church*, 130. I wish to thank my friend and colleague Clay Kannard for pointing me to the importance of these grammars for evangelism.
10. Keller, *Center Church*, 131.
11. Daniel Strange, *Making Faith Magnetic: Five Hidden Things Our Culture Can't Stop Talking about . . . and How to Connect Them to Christ* (Epsom: The Good Book Company, 2021). One needs to be aware

that Strange draws and develops the five points from the work of Dutch missiologist Johan Herman Bavinck (1895–1964), whose many years of missionary experience in Indonesia have been a source of precious missiological insights.

12. Strange, *Making Faith Magnetic*, 27.
13. Strange, *Making Faith Magnetic*, 88.
14. Strange, *Making Faith Magnetic*, 89.
15. Strange, *Making Faith Magnetic*, 93.
16. Mark Gilbert with Cecily Paterson, *The Road Once Travelled: Fresh Thoughts on Catholicism* (Kingsford: Matthias Media, 2010), 56–57.
17. Galea, *Nothing in My Hand I Bring*, 27.
18. Timothy Keller, *The Prodigal God: Recovering the Heart of the Christian Faith* (London: John Murray Press, 2009).
19. Luca Diotallevi, *Fine corsa. La fine del Cristianesimo come religione confessionale* (Bologna: EDB, 2017).
20. Books containing testimonies of conversion from Roman Catholic backgrounds include Richard Bennett and Martin Buckingham, eds., *Far from Rome, Near to God: The Testimonies of 50 Converted Catholic Priests* (Portland, OR: Associated Publishers & Authors, 1994); Richard Bennett and Glenn Diehl, eds., *On the Wings of Grace Alone: The Testimonies of Thirty Converted Roman Catholics* (Port St. Lucie, FL: Solid Ground Christian Books, 2015); and Mark Gilbert, ed., *Stepping Out in Faith: Former Catholics Tell Their Stories* (Kingsford: Matthias Media, 2012).

Chapter 4

1. On the Roman Catholic doctrine of regeneration, see my *Same Words, Different Worlds: Do Roman Catholics and Evangelicals Believe the Same Gospel?* (London: IVP, 2021), 49–53.
2. Francis Schaeffer, *Plan for Action: An Action Alternative Handbook for "Whatever Happened to the Human Race?"* (Old Tappan, NJ: Fleming H. Revell, 1980), 68. Schaeffer spoke about co-belligerence in the second

chapter of his book *The Church at the End of the Twentieth Century* (1970), various editions.

3. Catholica, *Cum ecclesia et cum mundo* (Padova: Messaggero, 2004). In this book, Scognamiglio argues for an inclusivist and absorbing meaning of what it means for the Roman Catholic church to be "catholic."

4. https://isthereformationover.com/ (accessed June 26, 2024).

5. See my *A Christian's Pocket Guide to Mary: Mother of God?* (Fearn: Christian Focus, 2017).

6. More on this in Leonardo De Chirico and Mark Gilbert, eds., *The Nicene Creed: Can Evangelical and Roman Catholics Profess It Together?* (Kingsford: Matthias Media, 2024).

7. More on this in my *Same Words, Different Worlds*, 46–49.

8. Italian Evangelical Alliance, "An Evangelical Approach Towards Understanding Roman Catholicism," *European Journal of Theology* X (2001): 32–35.

Appendix 1

1. This sermon was preached at the church Breccia di Roma on March 19, 2017, on the occasion of the five hundredth anniversary of the Protestant Reformation and as part of a series of sermons on the five "Solus-Sola" of the evangelical faith: scripture alone, grace alone, faith alone, Christ alone, and to God alone be glory.

2. Martin Luther, *Small Catechism* (1529), "The Second Article: Redemption," https://catechism.cph.org/en/creed.html (accessed June 28, 2024).